Caroline County, Virginia

Order Book

1772–1773

Ruth and Sam Sparacio

HERITAGE BOOKS
2018

HERITAGE BOOKS
AN IMPRINT OF HERITAGE BOOKS, INC.

Books, CDs, and more—Worldwide

For our listing of thousands of titles see our website
at
www.HeritageBooks.com

Published 2018 by
HERITAGE BOOKS, INC.
Publishing Division
5810 Ruatan Street
Berwyn Heights, Md. 20740

International Standard Book Number
Paperbound: 978-1-68034-936-8

CAROLINE COUNTY, VIRGINIA
ORDERS
1772-1776

(This book is the first part of Caroline County Order Book 1772-1776. The pages are torn and much is missing. The page numbers are a guess most being missing.)

p   Caroline County May Court 1772
1   - RICHARD HIPKINS Plt. against ALEXANDER SPOTSWOOD Deft.
Came the parties by their Attorneys and the Defendant pleads Non Assumpsit which the Plantif joins and the trial thereof is referred til the next Court

      - JAMES MILLER Gent., Plantif against HENRY WINSLOW, Defendant   In Case
Came the parties by their Attorneys and the Defendant relinquishing his plea acknowledges the Plantifs action so far as to Five pounds, three shillings current money; It is therefore considered by the Court that the Plantif recover against the said Defendant the aforesaid sum of Five pounds three shillings by the Defendant in manner and form aforesaid confessed together with his costs by him in this behalf expended and the said Deft. in mercy &c.

      - The Exors of CHARLES GOODALL deced., against WILLIAM FLIPPO   On Petition
Continued for Defendant

      - JOHN GRAHAM & COMPANY Plts. against the Exors. of WM JOHNSTON deced.,
Deft. On Writ of Scirefacias   Continued for Defendant

      - JOHN ELLIOT PAYNE. Admor. of JOHN LEDFORD deced. Plt. against ANDREW HARRISON Defendant   In Case   Came the parties by their Attorneys & the Defendant pleads Not Guilty with leave which the Plantif joined and the trial thereof is referred til the next Court

      - Ordered BENJAMIN GLANTON pay JOHN JETER Three hundred and fifty pounds of tobacco for attending this Court fourteen days as an Evidence for him against MICA (missing)

      - Ordered CATHERINE MICOU pay PHILLIP JONES three hundred and fifty pounds of tobacco for attending this Court (missing) days as an evidence for her at the suit of BEN(missing)

p.   Caroline County May Court 1772
2   - Ordered that BENJAMIN GLANTON pay JOHN (missing) hundred and seventy
nine pounds (missing) attending this Court eleven days (missing) coming and returning Twenty four miles as an evidence for him against CATHERINE (missing)

      - (missing) EVELL against (missing) SNODGRASS.

      - On the motion of the Defendant by his Attorney, a Commission is awarded him to take the Deposition of WILLIAM WHITFIELD who is about to depart this Colony debene esse giving reasonable notice to the Petitioner of the time & place appointed for taking the same

      - JOHN ALEXANDER against JOHN DISMUKES   On Petition
Came the parties by their Attorneys & on hearing the evidences & arguments on both sides, It is considered by the Court that the Petitioner recover against the said Defendant One pound seven shillings and six pence, the Debt in the Petition specified. also his costs in this behalf expended

      - Ordered JOHN ALEXANDER pay JOHN ALEXANDER JUNR., One hundred and fifty three pounds of tobo; for attending this Court three days and once coming and returning twenty six miles as an Evidence for him against JOHN DISMUKES

p.   <u>Caroline County May Court 1772</u>
3   - JOHN SUTTON Plantif against WILLIAM HARRISON Defendant
Came the parties by their Attorneys (missing) having plead, On motion of the
Plantif time is granted him til the next Court to reply
        - Ordered JAMES STEWART pay THOMAS JONES (missing) hundred and twenty five
pounds of tobacco for attending this Court thirteen days as an Evidence for (missing)
against WILLIAM HARRISON
        - Ordered that the Court be adjourned til the Court in Course
        - The Minutes of the preceding Orders were signed by
                                        EDMUND PENDLETON Gent.

(The remainder of this page is blank.)

p   <u>Caroline County June Court 1772</u>
4   - ANDREW THOMPSON & COMPY. Plantifs against JOHN RIDING Defendant
JOHN SKINKER Gent. entered himself Special Bail for the Defendant according to
Law
        - On motion of JAMES CONDUIT who having taken the Oath prescribed by Law,
Certificate for obtaining Letters of Administration on the Estate of NATHANIEL CONDUIT
deceased which remained unadministered by THOMAS CONDUIT deceased is granted him.
Bond acknowledged & ordered to be recorded
        - Ordered EDMUND PENDLETON JUNR., BENJAMIN HUBBARD, JOHN WALDEN and
ANDREW HARRISON or any three of them (being first sworn) do appraise the Estate of
NATHANIEL CONDUIT deceased and return an Inventory to the Court
        - (missing) appearing to the Court that SAMUEL HARGRAVE is excused (missing)
Presentment of the Grand Jury found against him for not keeping his Road in repair
accor-ding to Law
        - (missing) and Certificate of Mrs. ELIZABETH MILLER, Wife of (missing) acknow-
ledgment of a Deed from her Husband & self (missing)turned & ordered to be recorded
        - (missing) THOMAS, JOHN WRIGHT, ROBERT LANCASTER and WILLIAM (missing)
of them (being first sworn) do appraise the Estate of (missing) that lies in ORANGE
County and return (missing) Court. the former Order set aside
        - (missing) ROBERT TALIAFERRO Gent. to JAMES REYNOLDS (missing) to be recorded
        - The Executors of WALTER CHILES deced., Plts. against (missing) Defendt. On
 Replevy Bond.(only portions of this entry appear)

p.   <u>At a Court held for Caroline County the Eleventh day of June one thousand</u>
5   <u>seven hundred and seventy two</u>
                        Present His Majesties Justices
        EDMUND PENDLETON   JOHN ARMISTEAD
        JAMES TAYLOR   WILLIAM BUCKNER   Gent.
        WALKER TALIAFERRO   and
        THOMAS LOWRY   JAMES UPSHAW

        - A Deed Indented and Receipt from JOHN JOHNSON (missing)GARET his Wife (she
being first privately examined) acknowledged and ordered to be recorded
        - WILLIAM SOUTHWORTH is appointed Overseer of the Road (missing) in room of
MATTHEW CRANK
        - An Assignment of ELIZABETH COMER's Dower returned to the Court and ordered
to be recorded
        - On the Petition of LEE ROY HIPKINS for leave (missing) Road leading by his

House, Ordered that THOMAS (missing) Gent., JAMES DANIEL & JOHN MARTIN (being first (missing) the conveniences and inconveniences that may (missing) alteration and report to Court

    - A Deed Indented and Receipt from JOHN (missing) QUARLES proved as to the Deed by the Oaths of (missing) SAMUEL REDD & BENJAMIN TOMPKINS (missing) BENJAMIN TOMPKINS which are (missing)

    - EDWARD POWERS Plantif against THOMAS CALA( ) Defendant

(Most of this entry is missing as is what appears to be another entry on this page)

(Pages seven through 14 appear to be missing, page numbers appear beginning with page 15.)

p.	Caroline County Court 11th of June 1772
15	- JOHN PENN Plt. against THOMAS BUSH Deft. Motion on Replevy Bond

Came as well the Plantif by his Attorney as the Defendant in his proper person and the said Defendant agrees that Judgment should be entered against him according to Bond; It is therefore considered by the Court that the Plantif recover against the said Defendant the Penalty of said Bond to be discharged by the payment of (blank) with legal interest from the (blank) til paid and the costs of this motion

    THOMAS PENNINGTON against ROBERT MONTH   In Debt

JAMES BOWIE JUNR. entered himself Special Bail for the Defendant according to Law

    - A Deed Indented & Receipt from JOHN TAYLOR Gent. to JOSEPH RITCHESON proved by the Oath of ROBERT MICKLEBERRY, BENJA: BOUGHAN & WILLIAM SOUTH-WORTH & ordered to be recorded

    - PATRICK DELANEY Plt. againt JOHN LOVELL & JOHN CRAWLEY, Defts.

Motion on Replevy Bond   The Defendant who had legal notice of this motion being solemnly called failed to appear; On motion of the Plantif a (missing) ment is granted him against the said Defendant for Seven pounds, the penalty of the said Bond to be discharged by the payment of Three pounds nine shillings & ten pence with legal Interest from the 25th day of January one thousand seven hundred and seventy two til paid and the costs of this motion

    - Present ROBERT GILCHRIST and JAMES MILLER Gent.

    - WILLIAM PICKETT against (missing)NAH HERNDON   On Petition

Pursuant to an award made and returned, It is considered by the Court that the Plantif recover against one pound twelve shillings and four pence, also his costs in this behalf expended

p.	Caroline County Court 11th of June 1772
16	- An Account of DAVID and PEYTON STERN's Executorship of the Estate of CHARLES STERN deceased returned & admitted to Record

    - Ordered that ANTHONY THORNTON & WALKER TALIAFERRO Gent. in conjunction with WILLIAM WOODFORD, JOHN BUCKNER & JOHN THORNTON Gent., who were formerly appointed or any two of them to view the Warehouses at CONWAYs and report to Court the proportion of Rents that ought to be between the Proprietor & County

    - On the Petition of SETH THORNTON Gent. setting forth that he has adjoining his land a good stream for a Water Grist Mill and prays that an acre of land on opposite of the said Run may be laid off for that purpose; It is ordered that the Sherif summon twelve Freeholders of the Vicinage who being met and duly sworn before a Majestrate or the Sherif shall diligently view & examine the lands adjacent thereto on both sides of the Run which may be affected or laid under water by building such Mill, together with the Timber & other conveniences thereon and that they report specially the true value of the acre petitioned for and the conveniences & inconveniences and the damages to the parties hold the same or to any other person or persons whatsoever under their hands & seals

- Ordered WILLIAM PICKETT pay MESS PICKETT one hundred and twenty five pounds of tobacco for attending this Court five days as an Evidence for him against HANNAH HERNDON

- Ordered WILLIAM PICKETT pay ELIZABETH PICKETT one hundred and fifty pounds of tobacco for attending this Court six days as an Evidence for him against HANNAH HERNDON

- A Deed Indented & Receipt from ANTHONY THORNTON, WILLIAM FLEET, BAYLOR WALKER & ELIZABETH SIMPLE, JOHN ELLIOT PAYNE & MARY his Wife (she being first privately examined) to JOSEPH ELLIOT PAYNE acknowledged by ANTHONY THORNTON, WILLIAM FLEET, JOHN ELLIOT PAYNE & MARY his Wife & ordered to be recorded

- Present SAMUEL HAWES Gent.

- PATTY MANN against JOHN SUTTON   On Petition for Freedom
Came the parties by their Council & on hearing the same it is considered by the Court that the Petition be dismissed

- A Deed indented from THOMAS COLEMAN to JOHN (missing) proved by the Oaths of ANTHONY NEW, PAUL THILMAN and (missing) GUY and ordered to be recorded

(No pages numbered 17 and 18).

p.   Caroline County Court the 11th of June 1772
19   - A Deed indented & Receipt from ANTHONY THORNTON, WM. FLEET, BAYLOR WALKER & ELIZABETH SIMPLE, JOHN ELLIOT PAYNE & MARY his Wife (she being first privately examined) to DAVID SEAL acknowledged by ANTHONY THORNTON, WILLIAM FLEET, JOHN ELLIOT PAYNE & MARY his Wife & ordered to be recorded

- Two Bills of Sale from JOHN LOVELL to JOHN SMITH JUNR. acknowledged & ordered to be recorded

- An Inventory and Appraisement of the Estate of JOSEPH REYNOLDS deceased in Caroline County returned & ordered to be recorded

- A Deed indented & Receipt from RICHARD WOOLFOLK to MARTHA NODEN acknowledged & ordered to be recorded

- LAWRENCE LONG Plt. against JOHN GEORGE Hhd. Defendt.   In Case
Dismissed by Plantifs Note

- WILLIAM ALE JUNR. against RICHARD PEMBERTON Recogn: for Breach of the
Peace   Came the parties by their Attorneys & on hearing the same is dismissed

- JOHN SUTTON Plantif against WILLIAM STEVENS & BENJAMIN TOMPKINS Deft.
In Debt   Came the parties by their Attorneys and the Defendants agree that Judgment should be entered against them according to Bond; Therefore it is considered by the Court that the Plantif recover against the said Defendant Eighty one pounds Two shillings, the Debt in the Declaration mentioned together with his costs by him in this behalf expended; But this Judgment, except the costs, is to be discharged by the payment of Forty pounds eleven shillings currt. money with legal interest from the first day of April one thousand seven hundred and seventy two til paid; By consent, Execution on the Judgment is ordered to be stayed til October next

- An Inventory & Appraisement of the Estate of JAMES HURT deceased returned & ordered to be recorded

p   Caroline County Court 11th June 1772
20   - JOHN TENNANT Plt. against ISAC CARRICK Deft.   In Case
On motion of the Plantif by his Attorney, Judgment is granted against the said

Defendant for his costs by him in this behalf expended
- THOMAS JETT Gent., Plantif against JOHN ARMISTEAD Gent., Common Bail for JOHN FORTH. Defendant   In Debt.   Came the parties by their Attorneys and the Defendant relinquishing his plea acknowledges the Plantifs action; Therefore it is considered by the Court that the Plantif recover against the Defendant twelve pounds eight shillings and six pence currt. money, the Debt in the Declaration mentioned together with his costs in this behalf expended; And the said Defendant in mercy &c., But this Judgment except the costs is to be discharged by the payment of Six pounds four shillings and three pence with legal Interest from the first day of January one thousand seven hundred and Sixty seven til paid
- WILLIAM PARKER against MARY & WILLIAM BROWN, Executrix & Exor. of JOHN BROWN deced.,   On motion of the Plantif by his Attorney Judgment is granted him against the said Defendants for the costs by him in this behalf expended
- WILLIAM TOOMBS Plt. against GEORGE WEEDON Defendt.   In Case
By consent of parties, this suit is to be redocketed and referred to EDMUND PENDLETON, ANTHY THORNTON & WALKER TALIAFERRO Gt., or any two of them, whose award is to be entered the Judgment of this Court
- EUCLID WHITLOCK Plt. against FREDERICK FORTSON Deft.   In Case
Came the parties by their Attorneys & a Jury to wit THOMAS LAUGHLIN, Foreman, &c., who being sworn well and truly to try the matter on issue, do say that the Plantif hath sustained damages by reason of the said Defendant to Five pounds ten shillings currt. money; Therefore it is considered by the Court that the Plantif recover against the said Defendant his damages (the remainder of this entry is missing)

p.   At a Court continued and held for Caroline County the Twelvth day of June
21   one thousand seven hundred and seventy two
                      Present his Majesties Justices
          EDMUND PENDLETON   JAMES MILLER
          ROBERT GILCHRIST   and   Gent.
          JAMES TAYLOR   THOMAS LOWRY

- ALEXANDER BAINE Plantiff against WILLIAM HIGGIN Deft.   In Debt
Came the parties by their Attorneys & the Plantiff joined Demurrer of the Defendant & continued for Argument
- ALEXANDER BAINE Plantiff against WILLIAM HIGGIN Deft.   In Case
Came the parties by their Attorneys and the Defendant prays further leave til the next Court to consider of and answer the Plantifs writ & declaration which is granted him
- BURNLEY & BRACKENRIDGE Pltfs. against WILLIAM PERKINS Defendt.
In Case   Came the Plantifs by their Attorney and a Jury to wit LEE ROY HIPKINS Foreman &c., who being sworn well and truly to enquire the damages in this cause, do say that the Plantifs hath sustained damages by reason of the said Defendant to thirty five pounds fourteen shillings & seven pence currt. money; Therefore it is considered by the Court that the Plantifs recover against the said Defendant, FREDERICK & STEPHEN FORTSONs, Security for his appearance the aforesaid sum of Thirty five pounds fourteen shillings & seven pence currt. money by the Jurors in form aforesaid assessed together with their costs in this behalf expended and the said Defendant in mercy &c.

p   Caroline County Court 12th of June 1772
22   (On margin: This Judgment set aside)
            - JOHN PICKETT Plantiff against MOLLY ASHBURN & JOHN DOWNER Defendts.
In Debt   Came the parties by their Attorneys and the Defendants relinquishing
their plea acknowledge the Plantifs action. It is therefore considered by the Court that
the Plantif recover against the said Defendants Eighty one pounds eight shillings currt.
money, the Debt in the Declaration mentioned, together with all his costs by him in this
behalf expended; And the said Defendants in Mercy &c., This Judgment except the costs
is to be discharged by the payment of Forty pounds fourteen shillings currt. money
with legal Interest thereon from the twenty first day of January one thousand seven
hundred and seventy one til paid; By consent of the Plantif, the Defendants have leave
til the next Court to make appear any discounts before SAMUEL HAWES Gent.
            - JOHN SUTTON Plt. against RANDOLPH DEPRIEST Deft.   In Case
This suit abates by the death of the Plantif
            - JAMES EMMERSON Plantif against WILLIAM REYNOLDS, Defendant   In Case
Came the parties by their Attorneys and the Defendant relinquishing his plea acknowledges the Plantifs action. Therefore it is considered by the Court that the Plantif
recover against the Defendant Thirteen pounds ten shillings & eight pence, the Debt in
the Declaration mentioned, together with his costs by him in this behalf expended; and
the said Defendant in mercy &c., But this Judgment except the costs is to be discharged
by the payment of Six pounds eleven shillings & four pence currt. money with legal
Interest thereon from the 19th day of July one thousand seven hundred and seventy til
paid
            - THOMAS JETT, Assignee of HUBBARD & BAKER, Plt., against JOHN ARMISTEAD
Deft.   In Debt   On motion of the Plantif by his Attorney, Judgment is granted him
against the said Defendant for his costs by him in this behalf expended

p   Caroline County Court 12th of June 1772
23   - JOHN UPSHAW Gent., against YOUNGER PITTS   On Petition
            TheDefendant being duly summoned & failing to appear, tho solemnly called. On
motion of the Petitioner by his Attorney Judgment is granted him against the said Defendant for one pound fifteen shillings current money, the debt in the Petition specified, also his costs in this behalf expended. (On margin: 90 lbs. Nett Tobo: 7/6)
            - BENJAMIN BAKER against JOHN ACREY   On Petition
Came the parties by their Attorneys, & on hearing the Evidence & Arguments of each
party, it is considered by the Court that the Petitioner recover against the said Defendant Two pounds Ten shillings currt. money, also his costs by him in this behalf
expended. (On margin: 64 lbs. Nett Tobo: 7/6)
            - WILLIAM SOUTHWORTH against FREDERICK FORTSON   On Petition
The Defendant by his Attorney saith that he cannot deny the allegations of the
Petition. On motion of the Petitioner by his Attorney, Judgment is granted him against
the said Defendant for two pounds ten shillings & eight pence, the Debt in the Petition
specifified, also his costs by him in this behalf expended. (On margin: 60 lbs. Nett Tobo:
7/6.
            - NICHOLAS DARNALD Plt. against JOHN SCOTT Defendt.   On Debt
The Defendant being duly arrested and failing to appear tho solemnly called. On
motion of the Plantif by his Attorney, it is considered by the Court that the Plantif recover against the said Defendant and GEORGE MADDISON, security for his appearance,
six pounds currt. money with legal Interest from the first day of December 1770 til paid,
the Debt in the Declaration mentioned together with his costs by him in this behalf

expended, and the said Defendant in mercy &c., (On margin: 179 lbs. Tobo. 75 of it at 15/, or 150 lbs. of Tobo)

    - WILLIAM SEXTON againt CORNELIUS HUDDLESTON   On Petition
The former process in this suit not being executed, on motion of the Plantif by his Attorney, a new summons is awarded against the Defendant returnable to the next Court

p.   Caroline County Court 12th of June 1772
24   - ROBERT SCOTT Plantif against THOMAS BURK Defendt. In Case
    Came the parties by their Attorneys and a Jury, to wit, LEE ROY HIPKINS, foreman &c., who being sworn well and truly to inquire of the damages in this suit, do say that the Plantif sustained damages by reason of the said Defendant by Five pounds seventeen shillings & eight pence currt. mone; Therefore it is considered by the Court that the Plantif recover against the said Defendant and FREDERICK FORTSON, security for his appearance, the damages aforesaid by the Jurors in form aforesaid assessed together with his costs by him in this behalf expended and the said Defendants in mercy &c. (On margin: 251 lbs. of Tobo, 160 at 12/ remainder of it 15/ or 150 lbs. Tobo & 1/3)
    - ROBERT SCOTT Plantif against JAMES HEAD LYNCH Defendt. In Case
  Came the parties by their Attorneys and a Jury, to wit, LEE ROY HIPKINS foreman &c, who being sworn well and truly to inquire of damages in this suit, do say that the Plantif hath sustained damages by reason of the Defendant to Nine pounds nine shillings currt. money; It is therefore considered by the Court that the Plantif recover against the said Defendant his damages aforesaid by the Jurors in form aforesaid assessed together with his costs by him in this behalf expended, and the said Defendant in mercy &c., (On margin: 251 lbs. Tobo. 165 lbs. of it may be dischd> at 15/ or 150 lbs. Tobo: & 1/3)
    - ROBERT FERGUSON Plt. against CORNELIUS NOELL Defendt. In Debt
  This day came the Plantif by his Attorney and the Defendant being again solemnly called & failing to appear, it is considered by the Court the the Plantif recover against the said Defendant Ninety four pounds current money, the Debt in the Declaration specified, together with his costs by him in this behalf expended; and the said Defendant in mercy &c., But this Judgment except the costs is to be discharged by the payment of Thirty pounds four shillings & two pence with legal Interest thereon from the fifth day of March 1771 til paid
    - JOHN ELLIOT PAYNE Plantif against WILLIAM DUDLEY Defendt. In Case
Dismissed, agreed.

p.   Caroline County Court 12th of June 1772
25   - LOFLIN NEWMAN Plt. against JOHN WILY Defendt. On Writ of Scirefacias
    The Defendant being duly warned and failing to appear tho solemnly called, On motion of the Plantif by his Attorney, Judgment is granted him against the said Defendant for Twenty eight pounds eight shillings current money, the Debt in the said Writ specified, together with the costs by him in this behalf expended; and the said Defendant in mercy &c., But this Judgment except the costs is to be discharged by the payment of Fourteen pounds four shillings with legal Interest thereon from the twenty first day of May one thousand seven hundred and sixty five til paid (On margin: 112 lbs. tobo: 75 part of it at 1 1/2 the rest at 15/ or 150 lbs. tobo.)
    - CONSTANTINE SMITH against STEPHEN FORTSON   On Petition
  The Defendant being duly summoned and failing to appear tho solemnly called, On motion of the Petitioner by his Attorney, Judgment is granted him against the said Defendant for Seven hundred & twenty five pounds of tobacco, Eleven shillings and five

pence, sixty one pounds of tobacco and seven shillings and six pence, the Debt in the Petition specified, together with the costs by him in this behalf expended; (On margin: 76 lbs. N. Tobo: & 7/6)

- The Will of CHARLES LEWIS Gent., further proved by the Oath of JOHN TENNANT & ordered to be recorded
- ANTHONY HADEN Plt. against JOHN FARGUSON Deft.   In Debt
The former process in this suit not being executed, On motion of the Plantif by his Attorney, an Attachment is awarded him against the Estate of the said Defendant returnable to the next Court
- SAMUEL MAJOR Plantif against WILLIAM HARRISON, Defednt.   In Case
Came the parties by their Attorneys & the Defendant saving & reserving to himself all manner & advantage of exception as will to the Jurisdiction of the Court as to the Plantifs

p.   Caroline County Court 12th of June 1772
26   Writ and Declaration and prays times til the next Court to answer thereto which
          is granted him
- BENJAMIN JOHNSTON against PHILIP JOHNSTON, Admr. of THOS: JOHNSTON, Defendt.   In Debt   Came the parties by their Attorneys, and the Defendant prays oyer of this Writing Obligatory in the Declaration mentioned and time is granted him til next Court to answer the same
- BENJAMIN JOHNSTON Plt. against PHILLIP JOHNSTON, Defendt., Admor. of THOS. JOHNSTON   In Case   Came the parties by their Attorneys & saving and reserving to himself all manner & advantage of exception as well to the Jurisdiction of the Court as to the Plantifs Writ and Declaration and prays leave til the next Court to consider of and answer thereto which is granted him
- JOHN BAYLOR Esqr. Plt. against WILLIAM & MARY BROWN, Exr. & Exrx. of JOHN BROWN deced., In Debt   This suit abates by the Plantifs death
- JOHN BAYLOR Esqr. Plt. against WILLIAM BROUGHILL Defendt. In Debt This suit abates by the death of the Plantif
- JOHN BAYLOR Esqr. Plt. against JOHN BROUGHILL Defendt.   In Debt This suit abates by the Plantiff's death
- NICHOLAS WARE JUNR. against HENRY TERRILL   On Petition
The Defendant being duly summoned & failing to appear tho solemnly called, On motion of the Petitioner by his Attorney, Judgment is granted him against the said Defendant for three pounds fifteen shillings with legal Interest thereon from the first day of December 1770 til paid, the Debt in the Petition specified, also his costs in this behalf expended (On margin: 80 lbs. Tobo & 7/6)

p.   Caroline County Court 12th of June 1772
27   - NICHOLAS WARE JUNR. Plantif against JOHN PLANT Deft.   On Petition
          The Defendant being duly summoned and failing to appear tho solemnly called, On the motion of the Petitioner by his Attorney, Judgment is granted him against the said Defendant for Two pounds ten shillings currt. money, the Debt in the Petition specified together with his costs by him in this behalf expended, But this Judgment except the costs is to be discharged by the payment of One pound five shillings with legal Interest from the first day of October 1769 til paid
- NICHOLAS WARE JUNR. against DAVID HERNDON   On Petition
Dismissed, agreed
- NICHOLAS WARE JUNR. against JOHN MEACHEM   On Petition
The Defendant being duly summoned and failing to appear tho solemnly called, On

motion of the Petitioner by his Attorney, Judgment is granted him against the said Defendant for Five pounds currt. money, the specialty of the Bond, Tobo: to be discharged by the payment of Two pounds Ten shillings current money with legal Interest from the first day of October one thousand seven hundred and sixty nine til paid, also his costs in this behalf expended

- LEE ROY & SAMUEL HIPKINS, Exrs. of SAMUEL HIPKINS deced., against GEORGE MAJOR & SAML: MAJOR Defts.　　In Debt

The Defendants being arrested and failing to appear tho solemnly called, On motion of the Plantif by his Attorney, it is ordered that unless the Defendants appear at the next Court and answer the suit, Judgment be entered agaisnt them for what shall appear due the Plantifs & costs

- LEE ROY & SAML: HIPKINS Pltfs. against SAMUEL MAJOR & GEORGE ALSOP Defts.　On Petition　The Defendants being duly summoned & failing to appear

p. 　Caroline County Court 12th of June 1772
28 　　tho solemnly called, On motion of the Petitoner by his Attorney, Judgment is granted them against the said Defendant for Four pounds fifteen shillings the Debt in the Petition specified, also their costs in this behalf expended; But this Judgment except the costs is to be discharged by the payment of One pound eleven shillings & seven pence half penny with legal Interest from the 12th of April one thousand seven hundred & seventy one til paid (On margin: 90 lbs. Tobo; & 7/6)

- LEE ROY & SAML: HIPKINS,. Exrs. of SAML: HIPKINS deced., against DAVID WHITE & JOHN SCANDLAND　On Petition　The Defendants being duly summoned and failint to appear tho solemnly called, On motion of the Petitioner by his Attorney, Judgment is granted them against the said Defendant for Ten shillings currt. money, the Debt in the Petition specified, and their costs in this behalf expended; But this Judgment except the costs is to be discharged by the payment of Eleven shillings and three pence with legal Interest from the Eighth day of March 1770 til paid (On margin: 73 lbs. Tobo: & 7/6).

- LEE ROY & SAML: HIPKINS Plts. against JOHN BROWN Defent. In Debt
JAMES CONDUIT entered himself special Bail for the Defendant according to Law. Came the parties by their Attorneys and the Defendant prays Oyer of the Writing Obligatory in the Declaration mentioned which is granted & leave til next Court to answer thereto which is granted him

- FREDERICK FORTSON against JAMES GREGORY　　Assault & Battery
The former process in this suit not being executed, On motion of the Plantif by his Attorney, an Attachment is awarded him against the Estate of the said Defendant returnable to the next Court

- HOLT RICHESON, Admr. of CHARLES SEATON against PATRICK CAFRY & JOHN SUTTON　　On Petition　On motion of the Petitioner by his Attorney, Judgment is granted him against the said Defendants for his costs by him in this behalf expended

- The Honble. RICHARD CORBIN Esqr. Plt. against EDMUND JONES, WM: & MICAJAH JONES Defendts.　Trespass　　Dismissed

p. 　Caroline County Court 12th of June 1772
29 　- HUGH SAMPSON against WILLIAM CLAYTON　　On Petition
The Defendant being duly summoned & failing to appear tho solemnly called, On motion of the Petitioner by his Attorney Judgment is granted him against the said Defendant for One pound fifteen shillings with legal interest from the first day of November one thousand seven hundred & seventy one til paid, the Debt in the Petition specified, also his costs in this behalf expended. (On margin: 80 lbs. Tobo: & 7/6)

- MUSCOE GARNETT & COMPY. Plts. against FRANCIS CHANDLER Deft.   In Debt
The Defendant being duly arrested & failing to appear tho solemnly called, On motion
of the Plantifs by their Attorneys, it is ordered that unless the Defendant appears at the
next Court and answers this suit, Judgment will be entered against him & WILLIAM G.
JONES, security for his appearance, for what shall appear due the Plantifs & costs
- ROBERT PAYNE WARING against JOHN TURNER   On Petition
The Defendant being duly summoned & failing to appear tho solemnly called, On
motion of the Petitioner by his Attorney, Judgment is granted him against the said Defendant for three pounds ten shillings, the Debt in the Petition specified, and his costs
in this behalf expended (On margin: 60 lbs. Tobo & 7/6)
- THOMAS SHIP JUNR. Plt. against WILLIAM TOOMBS Deft.   On Debt
The Defendant being duly arrested and failing to appear tho solemnly called, On
motion of the Plantif by his Attorney, It is ordered that unless the Defendant appear at
the next Court and answer this suit, Judgment will be entered against him and JOHN
GRIFFIN, security for his appearance for what shall appear due the Plantif & costs
- The Same Plt. against The Same Deft.   In Case   The same order

p.   Caroline County Court 12th of June 1772
30   - ANN CLAYTON Plt. against THOMAS BURK Defendt.   On Petition
The Defendant being duly summoned & failing to appear tho solemnly called, On
motion of the Petitioner by her Attorney, Judgment is granted her against the said De-
fendant for One pound fifteen shillings, the Debt in the Petition specified, also her costs
in this behalf expended
- ELIJAH McKEE Plt. against JOHN MELEAR JUNR. Deft. Trespass, Assault &
Battery   This suit is continued
- ANTHONY & BETTY BOWCOCKs, Exr. & Exrs. of JAS: BOWCOCK deced., against
JOHN MELEAR JUNR. & JAMES JOHNSTON Defts.   In Debt
The Defendant being arrested and failing to appear tho solemnly called, On motion of
the Plantifs by their Attorney, It is ordered that unless the Defendants apepar at the
next Court and answer the suit, Judgment will be entered against them for what shall
apear due the Plantifs & costs
- ANTHONY & BETTY BOWCOCKs, Exr. & Exrs. of JAS: BOWCOCK deced. against
JOHN LONG & JAMES JOHNSTON Defendants   In Debt
The Defendant being arrested & failing to appear tho solemnly called, On motion of the
Plantifs by their Attorney, It is ordered that unless the Defendants appear at the next
Court & answer the suit, Judgment to be entered against them for what shall appear to
be due the Plantifs & costs
- EDWARD DIXON Plt. against JOHN BROUGHILL Defendt. On Petition
The Defendant being duly summoned and failing to appear tho solemnly called, on the
motion of the Petitioner by his Attorney, Judgment is granted him against the said
Defendant for Four pounds, the Debt in the Petition specified, also his costs in this
behalf expended
- BENJAMIN ISBELL Plt. against JAMES HURT Deft.   On Petition
Abates by Defendants death

p.   Caroline County Court 12th of June 1772
31   - DOCTOR WILLIAM JOHNSON, Plt. against RICHARD JOHNSON, Exr. of FRANCIS
COLEMAN deced., In Case   Came the parties by their Attorneys & the Defendant prays time til the next Court to consider of and answer the Plantifs Writ & Declaration which is granted him

- MESS PICKETT Plantiff against DANIEL BARKSDALE Defendt. In Case
Came the Plantif by his Attorney and a Jury, to wit, LEE ROY HIPKINS &c., who being
sworn well and truly to enquire the damages in this suit, do say that the Plantif hath
sustained damages by reason of the said Defendant to fifty four pounds current money.
It is therefore considered by the Court that the Plantif recover against the said Defendant and HENRY WARE, Security for his appearance, his damages aforesaid by the
Jurors in form aforesaid assessed together with his costs by him in this behalf expended; By consent of the Plt. the Defendant has leave to make appear any discounts
before JAMES TAYLOR Gent. RICHD. & JAMES JOHNSON or any two of them
- Report returned on LEE ROY HIPKINS Petition as followeth: Pursuant to an
Order of the Worshipfull Court of Caroline, we the Subscribers being first sworn viewed
the Road proposed to be turned by LEE ROY HIPKINS from RIDDLES SHOP leading by
DIGGS (   ) in the current Road to the DARK CHURCH and find that the New Road to be
seventeen yards nearer than the Old Road and in our opinion a much better way it
being level and shunning a bad hill the Old Road. Given under our hands this 9th day of
June One thousand seven hundred and seventy two; JAMES DANIEL, JOHN MARTIN,
THOMAS LOWRY. On considering the same, the Court do grant him liberty of opening it
agreeable to the Report
- WILLIAM SHACKELEFORD Plt. against HENRY MARTIN Defendt. On a Replevy
Bond The Defendant who had legal notice of this motion being so solemnly called &
failing to appear. On lthe motion of the Plantif by his Attorney, Judgment is granted
him against the said Defendant for Seventy eight pounds seven shillings, the Penalty of
the said Bond: to be discharged by the payment of Fourteen pounds eight shillings & six
pence with legal Interest from the 20th day of Febry: 1772 til paid and the cost of this
motion

p.   Caroline County Court 12th of June 1772
32   - HENRY STEWART Plt. against AMBROSE BLACKBURN Deft., On Attachment
Came the Plantif by his Attorney and MARY FLETCHER. the Garnishee in the suit,
having (agreeable to Order of this Court) declared before a Majestrate that the Defendant is entitled one fourth part of her Father, ELIAS BLACKBURN deced. personal Estate
which she has in her possession and the said Defendant being being solemnly called
failed to appear and replevy the same; It is considered by the Court that the Plantif recover against the said Defendant the sum of Thirty pounds, also his costs in this behalf
expended & the Defendant in Mercy &c., Ordered that THOMAS LOWRY & JAMES UPSHAW
Gent., settle with MARY FLETCHER, the Garnishee, her account of administration on the
Estate of ELIAS BLACKBURN deceased and report to Court what part of the Estate the Defendant is intitled to under the Will of the said ELIAS BLACKBURN deceased
- Ordered that MESS PICKETT pay THOMAS REYNOLDS one hundred and fifty
pounds of tobacco for attending this Court six days as an evidence for him against
BARKSDALE
- Ordered that MESS PICKETT pay WILLIAM PICKETT two hundred and seventy
five pounds of tobacco for attending this Court Eleven days as an Evidence for him
against BARKSDALE
- Ordered that HENRY STEWART pay JOHN TURNER two hundred and seventy five
pounds of tobacco for attending this Court Eleven days as an Evidence for him against
BLACKBURN
- Ordered that HENRY STEWART pay JAMES FLETCHER fifty pounds of tobacco for
attending this Court two days as an Evidence for him against BLACKBURN

- JAMES WRIGHT Plt. against WILLIAM JOHNSTON Deft.
On Motion of the Plantif by his Attorney, Judgment is granted him against the said
Defendant for his costs by him in this behalf expended

p.   Caroline County Court 12th of June 1772
33   - WILLIAM AYLETT & JAMES RUSSELL, Admors. of JOHN RUSSELL deced.,
        against WILLIAM SUTTON   On Petition   By consent of the parties by their
Attorneys, all matters in difference between them relative this Petition is referred to
the determination of JOHN HILL, Gent., whose award is to be returned and entered as the
Judgment of this Court & it is also agreed that if either shall fail to attend at the time &
place appointed for hearing the same, that the Referee proceed without the party so
failing, provided he has legal notice thereof
        - The Trustees of the Honble: WM; BYRDs Lottery Complts. against ROBT. &*
BENJA: JOHNSTON, Exors. of WM: JOHNSTON deced., Defts.   In Chy.
The former process in this suit not being executed, on motion of the Compts. by their
Council, a new summons is awarded them returnable to the next Court
        - HOLT RICHESON, Admor. of CHARLES SEATON deced., Plt.   against
ROBERT SCOTT Defendt.   In Case   By consent of parties, by their Attorneys,
all matters in difference between them relative to this suit referred to the determination of RICHD: SQUIRE TAYLOR, JEREMIAH RAWLINGS & GEORGE GUY, Gent., or any two
of them whose award is to be returned & entered the Judgment of this Court
        - JOSEPH DOODY against ROBERT WOOLFOLK Deft.   On Petition
The Defendant being duly summoned and failing to appear tho solemnly called, On
motion of the Petitioner by his Attorney, Judgment is granted him against the said Defendant for One pound fifteen shillings, the Debt in the Petition specified, together
with his costs by him in this behalf expended
        - JOHN GRAY & COMPY,. Plts. against JOHN JOHNSON   In Case
JOHN JONES entered himself Special Bail for the Defendant according to Law. Came the
parties by their Attorneys and the Defendant prays leave til the next Court to consider
of & answer the Plantiff's Writ & Declaration which is granted him

p.   Caroline County Court 12th of June 1772
34   - JOHN GRAY & COMPY. Plts. against JOHN GOODRICH Defendt. In Debt
        The Defendant being arrested & failing to appear tho solemnly called, On motion
of the Plantifs by their Attorneys, It is ordered that unless the Defendant appears at the
next Court and answer this suit, Judgment to be entered against him & JOHN ARMISTEAD
Gent., security for his appearance, for what shall appear due the Plantifs and costs
        - The Same Plts. against The Same Defendts.   In Case
The same order as last
        - THOMAS MOORE's Trustees, Plts. against JOHN BAYLOR Gent. Defendant In Case
This suit abates by the death of the Defendant
        - THOMAS MOORE's Trustees Plts. against JOHN ARMISTEAD Gent., Defendt. In Case
Came the parties by their Attorneys and the Defendant prays leave till the next Court
to consider of and answer the Plantifs Writ & Declaration which is granted him
        - JAMES JOHNSTON against FREDERICK FORTSON   On Petition
The Defendant being duly summoned and failing to appear tho solemnly called, On
motion of the Petitioner by his Attorney, Judgment is granted him against the said
Defendant for Two pounds, the Debt in the Petition specified, also his costs by him in
this behalf expended

- ELIZABETH SAMUEL Plt. against JOHN SULLENGER Deft.   In Case
Came the parties by their Attorneys and the Defendant prays leave til the next Court to
consider of & answer the Plantifs Writ and Declaration which is granted him
- JOHN TAYLOR & JOHN PENN, Plts. against   RICHARD JERVICE Defendt. In Debt
Came the parties by their Attorneys & the Defendant pleads payment which the Plantif
joined & the trial thereof is referred til the next Court

p   Caroline County Court 12th of June 1772
35   - Ordered that SAMUEL MEREDITH pay RALPH GOUGH MEREDITH Nine hundred
          and five pounds of tobacco for attending this Court five days and four times
coming & returning Sixty five miles as an Evidence for him against HOLLIDAY
- Ordered that JOHN HOLLIDAY pay JOHN MITCHELL five hundred and sixty five
pounds of tobacco for attending this Court thirteen days and five times coming & returning sixteen miles as an Evidence for HOLLIDAY at the suit of MEREDITH
- EDWARD DIXON & JOHN SKINKER Gent., Exors. of THS: TURNER deced. against
BENJAMIN HUBBARD Gent., Defendant   In Debt   Came the parties by their
Attorneys & the Defendant relinquishing his plea acknowledges the Plantiffs action,
Therefore it is considered by the Court that the Plantif recover agaisnt the said Defen-
dant Four hundred pounds current money, the Debt in the Declaration mentioned, toge-
ther with their costs in this behalf expended; and the said Defendant in Mercy &c., but
this Judgment except the costs is to be discharged by the payment of twelve pounds
seventeen shillings & eleven pence half penny with Interest from the seventh day of
March 1771 til paid
- RICHARD JOHNSTON, Exor. of FRANCIS COLEMAN against DAVID STERN
Defendt.   In Case   This Suit is dismissed, agreed
- The Same against the Same   On Petition
The Defendant being duly summmoned and failing to appear tho solemnly called, On
motion of the Petitioner by his Attorney, Judgment is granted him against the said De-
fendant for One pounds thirteen shillings & seven pence with legal Interest from the
15th day of December one thousand seven hundred and Sixty six til paid, the Debt in the
Petition specified; together with his costs by him in this behalf expended
- The Same against GRIFFIN CARTER   In Case   Dismissed agreed

p.   Caroline County Court 12th of June 1772
36   - RICHARD JOHNSTON, Executor of FRANCIS COLMAN deceased, against
          WILLIAM GUTHRIE   In Case   By consent of parties, all matters in dif-
ference between them relative this Writ is referred to the final determination of JAMES
TAYLOR & WILLIAM BUCKNER JUNR., Gent., whose award is to be returned & entered the
Judgment of this Court
- The Same Plt. against JAMES CARTER Defendt.   In Case
The same Order as last
- The Same against JOHN BOWCOCK   On Petition
The same Order as last
- The Same Plt. against JOHN LONG Deft.
The Defendant being arrested & failing to appear tho solemnly called, On motion of the
Petitioner by his Attorney it is ordered that unless the Defendant appear at the next
Court and answer this suit, Judgment be entered against him and RICHARD ROY, Secur-
ity for his appearance for what shall appear due the Plantif and costs
- The Same Plt. against THOMAS PICKETT Deft.   In Case
Came the Plantif by his Attorney & the Defendant failing to appear tho solemnly

called. On motion of the Plantif it is ordered that unless the Defendant appear at the next Court and answer this suit, Judgment be entered against him & THOMAS RIDDLE, Security for his appearance, for what shall aoppear to be due the Plantif & costs

    - The Same Plt. against WILLIAM JOHNSTON Doctor, Defendt. In Case
The former process in this suit not being executed, On motion of the Plantif by his Attorney, a new Writ is awarded him returnable to the next Court

    - The Same against JOHN RAGAN   In Case   Dismissed, agreed

p.   Caroline County Court 12th of June 1772
37   - RICHARD JOHNSTON, Exor. of FRANCIS COLEMAN deced., against   JOHN
    GRIFFIN Defendant In Case   The Defendant being arrested & failing to
appear tho solemnly called, On motion of the Plantif by his Attorney, it is ordered that unless the Defendant appear at the next Court & answer this suit, Judgment be entered against him for what shall appear to be due the Plantif & costs

    - The Same Plantiff against JOHN SANDERS JUNR. Deft. In Case
The Defendant being duly arrested & failing to appear tho solemnly called, On motion of the Petitioner by his Attorney, It is ordered that unless the Defendant appear at the next Court and answer this suit, Judgment be entered against him for what shall appear due the Plantif & costs

    - The Same Plt. against GARROTT HACKETT Deft. In Case
ROBERT MICKLEBERRY entered himself Special Bail for the Defendant according to Law. Came the parties by their Attorneys, and the Defendant prays leave til next Court to consider of and answer the Plantifs Writ & Declaration which is granted him

    - The Same Plts. against JOHN THILMAN Deft.   In Case
The same Order as last

    - The Same Plt. against PETER LANTOR Deft.   On Petition
The Defendant being duly summoned and failing to appear tho solemnly called, On motion of the Petitioner by his Attorney, Judgment is granted him against the said Defendant for Two pounds five & five pence half penny, the Debt in the Petition speci-fied, together with his costs by him in this behalf expended

    - The Same against NICHOLAS LANGFORD   On Petition
Dismissed

p.   Caroline County Court 12th of June 1772
38   - RICHARD JOHNSTON, Executor of FRAS: COLEMAN deced., against
    JOHN EVANS   On Petition   The Defendant being duly summoned & failing to
appear tho solemnly called, On motion of the Petitioner by his Attorney, Judgment is granted him against the said Defendant for One pound fourteen shillings & half penny the Debt in the Petition specified, and his costs in this behalf expended

    - The Same against JAMES ROBERTS   On Petition
the Defendant being duly summoned & failing to appear tho solemnly called, On motion of the Petitioner by his Attorney, Judgment is granted him against the said Defendant for one pound eleven shillings & ten pence, the Debt in the Petition speci-fied, also his costs in this behalf expended

    - The Same against GEORGE GIBSON   On Petition
The Defendant being duly summoned and failing to appear tho solemnly called, On motion of the Petitioner by his Attorney, Judgment granted him against the said Defen-dant for One pound fourteen shillings & one penny half penny, the Debt in the Petition specified also his costs in this behalf expended

    - The Same against WILLIAM GRAVES   On Petition
The Defendant being duly summoned and failing to appear tho solemnly called, On
motion of the Petitioner by his Attorney, Judgment is granted him againt the said Defendant for Two pounds thirteen shillings & nine pence half penny & the Debt in the
Petition specified, also his costs in this behalf expended
    - The Same against THOMAS BURK   On Petition
The Defendant being duly summoned & failing to appear tho solemnly called, On
motion of the Petitioner by his Attorney, Judgment is granted him against the said Defendant for Two pounds thirteen shillings & six pence three farthings, the Debt in the
Petition specified, also his costs in this behalf expended
    - The Same against WILLIAM REYNOLD   On Petition
Dismissed

p.   Caroline County Court 12th of June 1772
39   - RICHARD JOHNSTON, Executor of FRANCIS COLEMAN deced., against
    ELLIOT EMMERSON   On Petition   The former process in this suit not being
executed, on the motion of the Petitioner by his Attorney, a new summons is awarded
him returnable to the next Court
    - The Same against FRANCIS FLEMING   On Petition
The Defendant being duly summoned & failing to appear tho solemnly called, On
motion of the Petitioner by his Attorney, Judgment is granted him against the said Defendant for One pound nine shillings & seven pence half penny, the Debt in the
Petition specified, also his costs in this behalf expended
    - The Same against JOHN FARGUSON   On Petition
The Defendant being duly summoned and failing to appear tho solemnly called, On
motion of the Petitioner by his Attorney, Judgment is granted him against the said Defendant for Two pounds nine shillings and three pence, the Debt in the Petition specified, also his costs in this behalf expended
    - The Same against JOHN GEORGE (Hhd.)   On Petition
The Defendant being suly summoned & failing to appear tho solemnly called, On
motion of the Petitioner by his Attorney, Judgment is granted him against the said
Defendant for Four pounds & a half penny, the Debt in the Petition specified, also his
costs in this behalf expended
    - The Same against ANTHONY ARNOLD   On Petition
This suit abates by the Sheriffs return
    - HUGH HOUSTON, Acting Executor of WM. HOUSTON deced., Plt. against
    LAWRENCE BATTAILE Gent., Defendt.   In Case
Dismissed agreed

p.   Caroline County Court 12th of June 1772
40   - LeROY & SAMUEL HIPKINS, Exors. of SAML: HIPKINS deced. against
    JOHN WONDRUM & JOHN CROUCHER   On Petition
The Defendants being duly summoned and failing to appear tho solemnly called, On
motion of the Petitioner by his Attorney, Judgment is granted them against the said
Defendant for one pound nine shilligns & one penny, with legal Interest from the first
day of September one thousand seven hundred & sixty nine til paid; the Debt in the
Petition specified, also his costs in this behalf expended
    - JOHN BULLARD against RICHARD SHIP   On Attachment
Came the Plantif by his Attorney & JOHN PENN, Gent., Attorney for the Defendant,
moved that the Attachment might be quashed. On hearing the arguments on both sides,

It is considered by the Court that the same be dismissed & that the Defendant recover of the Plt (blank) who was security that he should prosecute the same with effect his costs by him in this behalf expended

- SAMUEL MEREDITH Plantif against JOHN HOLLIDAY Defendant   In Case
Came the parties by their Attorney & a Jury, to wit, LeROY HIPKINS foreman &c., who being impanelled & sworn well & truly to try the matter on issue joined, do say that the Plantif hath sustained damages by reason of the said Defendant to Fifty pounds current money: Therefore it is considered by the Court that the Plantif recover against the said Defendant his damages by the Jurors in form aforesaid assessed, Together with his costs by him in this behalf expended, & the said Defendant in Mercy &c.

- DOCTOR WILLIAM JOHNSTON against WILLIAM JOHNSTON   On Petition
The Defendant personally appeared & sayth that he cannot deny the allegations of the Petition, Therefore on motion of the Plantif by his Attorney, Judgment is granted him against the said Defendt for three pounds two shillings & six pence, also his costs in this behalf expended

p   Caroline County Court 12th of June 1772
41   - HOLT RICHESON, Admor. of CHARLES SEATON deced., against WILLIAM
HARRISON Defendt. In Debt   Came the parties by their Attorneys and the Defendant relinquishing his plea acknowledges the Plantifs action; Therefore it is considered by the Court that the Plantif recover against the said Defendant Two hundred pounds current money, the Debt in the Declaration mentioned with his costs by him in this behalf expended, and the said Defendant in Mercy &c., But this Judgment except the costs is to be discharged by the payment of One hundred and thirty three pounds seventeen shillings and ten pence three farthings with legal Interest thereon from the first day of March one thousand seven hundred & seventy two til paid, By consent of the Plantif, the Defendant has leave to make any just discount

- Our Sovereign Lord the King Plt. against ANN TAYLOR, THOMAS PITMAN & JOHN MOUNTAGUE, Defts.   Grand Jury Presentment
For reasons appearing, it is considered by the Court that the Defendants be acquitted.

- The Same against JOHN POLLETT   Grand Jury Presentment
On motion of the Plantif by CHARLES ROBINSON, Gent., his Deputy Attorney, Judgment is granted him against the said Defendant for his costs by him in this behalf expended

- ELIJAH McGHEE Plt. against JOHN SANDERS JUNR. Defendt.,   Assault & Battery
Came the parties by their Attorneys, and the Defendant prays time til the next Court to consider of & answer the Plantifs Writ & Declaration which is granted him

- ANDREW HARRISON Plt. against JAMES TAYLOR Gent., Defendt.   In Case
Came the parties by their Attorneys and the Defendant saving & reserving to himself all advantage of Exception as well to the Jurisdiction of the Court as to the Plantifs Writ & Declaration & prays time til the next Court to answer thereto which is granted him

p.   Caroline County Court 12th of June 1772
42   - JOHN BRAND Plt. against DANIEL BARKSDALE Deft.   In Trespass
Came the parties by their Attorneys and the Defendant pleads Not Guilty which the Plantif joined & the trial thereof is referred to the next Court

- GEORGE WATKINS Plt. against JOHN GEORGE (Hhd) Deft.   On Petition
The Defendant being duly summoned & failing to appear tho solemnly called, On motion of the Plantif by his Attorney Judgment is granted him against the said Defendant for Two pounds with legal Interest from the Tenth day of July one thousand seven hundred and Sixty Eight til paid, the Debt in the Petition specified: also his costs in this behalf expended

- WILLIAM JOHNSTON Plt. against MARY WREN Deft.   In Case
By consent of the parties, JAMES TAYLOR, JOHN SKINKER & JAMES DUNLOP, Gent., in conjunction with the former Referees are appointed to settle all matters in difference between them relative to this suit, whose award or the award of any two is to be returned and entered the Judgment of this Court
- RICHARD HIPKINS Plt. against ALEXANDER SPOTSWOOD Deft.   In Case
Came the parties by their Attorneys and a Jury, to wit, JOHN BROADDUS foreman &c., who being impanelled and sworn well & truly to try the matter on issue joined, do say that the Plantif hath sustained damages by reason of the said Defendant to One hundred & two pounds eighteen shillings & ten pence current money, Therefore it is considered by the Court that the Plantif recover against the said Defendant his damages aforesaid by the Jurors in form aforesaid assessed, together with his costs by him in this behalf expended; By consent of the Plantif, execution on this Judgment is ordered to be stayed til September
- JOSEPH GATEWOOD against HENRY SMITH   On Petition
Abates return of the Sherif

p   Caroline County Court 12th of June 1772
43   - SAMUEL MAJOR JUNR. against THOMAS GAINES   On Petition
The Defendant being duly summoned and failing to appear tho solemnly called, On motion of the Petitioner by his Attorney, Judgment is granted him against the said Defendant for Three pounds, the Debt in the Petition specified, also his costs in this behalf expended
- JOHN CATHRAE Plt. against SAMUEL MATTHEWS Deft. In Debt
On motion of the Plantif by his Attorney, Judgment is granted him against the Defendant for his costs by him in this behalf expended
- MORDECAI BUCKNER Gent., Plantif against NATHAN HOLLAWAY & ANN MITCHELL Defts.   In Debt   SAMUEL HAWES JUNR., Gent., entered himself Special Bail for the Defedants according to Law and came as well the Plantif by his Attorney as the Defendants by Note from under their hands and agree that Judgment should be entered against them for what shall appear due; Therefore it is considered by the Court that the Plantif recover against the said Defendants, Ten pounds eleven shillings, the Debt in the Declaration mentioned, also his costs in this behalf expended & the said Defendants in Mercy &c., But this Judgment except the costs is to be discharged by the payment of five pounds five shillings & six pence with legal Interest from the first day of January 1768 til paid
- PHILLIP MAY Plantif against JOHN LOVELL Defendant   In Debt
On motion of the Plantif by his Attorney, Judgment is granted him against the said Defendant for his costs in this behalf expended
- JAMES WRIGHT agaisnt JOHN BOURNE   Assault & Battery
Came the parties by their Attorneys and the Defendant prays time til next Court to consider of & answer the Plantifs Writ & Declaration which is granted him

p.   Caroline County Court 12th of June 1772
44   - JOSEPH GATEWOOD against RICHARD WATERS   On Petition
Came the parties by their Attorneys & on hearing the Evidence & arguments of each party, It is considered by the Court that the same be dismissed and that the Defendant recover against the Petitioner his costs by him in this behalf expended
- GEORGE DABNEY & BENJA: CLEVIAS SPILLER, Admors. of WILLIAM SPILLER Gent., against LAZAROUS YARBROUGH   On Writ of Scirefacias

The Defendant being duly warned & failing to appear tho solemnly called, On motion
of the Plantif by his Attorney, Judgment is granted him against the said Defendant for
Twelve pounds & one pence half penny, one hundred & seventy nine pounds of tobacco,
fifteen shillings or 150 lbs. Tobo. and One hundred and Six pounds of Nett tobacco and
fifteen shillings or 150 lbs. of tobacco, the Debt in the said Writ specified, also their
costs in this behalf expended
    - The Same Plantifs against AARON JERVICE Deft.   On Writ of Scirefacias
The former Writ in this suit not being executed, On motion of the Plantifs by their
Attorney a new Writ is award them returnable to the next Court
    - NICHOLAS WARE against WILLIAM PLUNKETT   On Petition
The Defendant by Note from under his hand agrees that Judgment should be entered
against him according to Petition; On motion of the Petitioner by his Attorney, Judgment is granted him against the said Defendant for Four hundred & thirty seven pounds
of tobacco & one pound eight shillings & six pence half penny by account & the Debt in
the Petition specified, also his costs by him in this behalf expended
    - Ordered that RICHARD WATERS pay MESS PICKETT JUNR. Two hundred pounds
of tobacco for attending this Court eight days as an Evidence for him at the suit of
GATEWOOD

p   Caroline County Court 12th of June 1772
45   - JOSEPH DEGARNETT Plantiff against WILLIAM TURNER Defendt. In Case
    On motion of the Plantif by his Attorney, Judgment is granted him against the
said Defendant for his costs by him in this behalf expended
    - THOMAS TARRANT Plt. against JOSEPH DEGARNETT Defendt.   In Case
Came the parties by their Attorneys, and the Defendant saving & reserving to himself
all manner and advantage of exception as well to the Jurisdiction of the Court as to the
Plantifs Writ & Declaration, & prays leave til the next Court to consider of & answer
thereto which is granted him
    - Messrs. ROBERT & ROBERT BOGLEs SCOTT & COMPY, Plantifs against RICHARD
JOHNSTON, Admor. of FRANCIS COLEMAN deced., Defendt.,   In Case
Came the parties by their Attorneys & the Defendant prays leave til the next Court to
consider of & answer the Plantifs Writ & Declaration which is granted him
    - REUBIN HERNDON Complt. against JOHN NORMENT Defendant In Chancery
Came the parties by their Council and the Defendant prays leave til the next Court to
consider of & answer the Plantifs Bill which is granted him
    - BARTHOLOMEW CHOWNING against BENJAMIN WILLIAMSON On Attachment
Dismissed
    - RICHARD JOHNSTON, Exor. of FRAS: COLEMAN against RUTH DISMUKES, Exrx. of
JAS: DISMUKES On Petition   Dismissed
    - THOMAS ROSE against FRANCIS DURRETT On Petition   Dismissed

p.   Caroline County Court 12th of June 1772
46   - RICHARD JOHNSTON, Exor. of FRANCIS COLEMAN deced., against GEORGE
MAJOR   On Petition   The Defendant being duly summoned & failing to
appear tho solemnly called, On motion of the Petitioner by his Attorney, Judgment is
granted him against the said Defendant for Four pounds twelve shillings nine pence
farthing, the Debt in the Petition specified, also his costs in this behalf expended
    - JOHN WEST against JOHN BEVERIDGE   On Petition
The Defendant being duly summoned and failing to appear tho solemnly called, On
motion of the Petitioner by his Attorney, Judgment is granted him against the said

Defendant One hundred and twenty nine pounds of tobacco & seven shillings & six pence, the Debt in the Petition specified, also his costs in this behalf expended
- WILLIAM CLAYTON Plt. against MATTHEW GALE JUNR., Defendt.   In Debt
Came as well the Plantif by his Attorney & the Defendant by Note from under his hand agrees that Judgment should be entered agst. him according to Note; It is therefore ordered by the Court that the Plantif recover against the said Defendant five pounds seven shillings with legal Interest from the first day of June 1770 til paid, the Debt in the Declaration mentioned, also his costs in this behalf expended and the said Defendant in Mercy &c.
- ANN HART Plantif against JEREMIAH PEIRCE Defendt.   In Case
Came the parties by their Attorneys and the Defendant saving & reserving to himself all advantage of exception as well to the Jurisdiction of the Court as to the Plantifs Writ & Declaration & prays leave til the next Court to consider of & answer thereto which is granted him
- ROBERT GARROTT Plantif against THOMAS SAMUELL Defendt.   In Case
Came the parties by their Attorneys, and the Defendant saving & reserving to himself all advantage of exception

p.   Caroline County Court 12th of June 1772
47   as well to the Jurisdiction of the Court as to the Plantifs Writ & Declaration, & prays time til the next Court to consider of & answer thereto, which is granted him
- MARY FLETCHER, Exrx. of ELIAS BLACKBURN deced., against ROBERT CHAPMAN & WILLIAM HORD Defendants   On Petition
The Defendants being duly summoned & failing to appear tho solemnly called, On motion of the Petitioner by her Attorney, Judgment is granted her against the said Defendants for Three pounds twelve shillings, the Debt in the Petition specified, together with her costs by her in this behalf expended, & this Judgment except the Costs to be discharged by the payment of Twelve shillings and three pence with legal Interest from the fifteenth day of November 1771 til paid
- The Same Plt. against HENRY MARTIN & RICHD: GOULDMAN   In Debt
Abates by return of Sheriff
- JOHN (AL--) against ELIJAH McKEE   On Petition
Came the parties by their Attorneys & on hearing the arguments of each party, It is considered by the Court that the same be dismissed & that the Defendant recover agaisnt the said Petitioner his costs by him in this behalf expended
- OWEN CARTER Plantif against JOHN GOODRICH Defendt.   Assault & Battery
The Defendant being arrested & failing to appear tho solemnly called, On motion of the Plantif by his Attorney, It is ordered that unless the Defendant appear at the next Court & answer this suit, Judgment be entered against him for what shall appear to be due the Plantif & costs
- ROBERT GILCHRIST Gent., Plaintiff against CHARLES STERNs Executors Defendts.   In Case   Came the parties by their Attorneys and the Defendant prays time til the next Court to consider of & answer the Plantifs Writ & Declaration which is granted him

p.   Caroline County Court 12th of June 1772
48   - GEORGE DABNEY & BENJAMIN CLEVIAS SPILLER, Administrators of WILLIAM SPILLER deceased, Plts., against WILLIAM JOHNSTON Defendt.   On Writ of Scirefacias   The Defendant being duly warned & failing to appear tho solemnly

called, On motion of the Plantiffs by their Attorney Judgment is granted them against the said Defendant for Twenty pounds Ten shillings & three pence half penny, with legal Interest from the eighth day of June one thousand seven hundred & sixty four til paid: Sixty five pounds of nett tobacco, the Debt in the said Writ mentioned; also their costs in this behalf expended, and the said Defendant in Mercy &c.

    - JAMES LANG Plt. against HENRY MARTIN Defendant   In Case
The Defendant being arrest & failing to appear tho solemnly called, On motion of the Plantif by his Attorney, It is ordered that unless the Defendant appear at the next Court & answer this suit, Judgment be entered agaisnt him, ISRAEL SNEED & JAMES GAUNT, securitys for his appearance for what shall appear due the Plantifs & costs

    - LEWIS TAYLOR, Assignee of HENRY LYNE Plt. against HENRY MARTIN & JOHN MARTIN Defendts.   In Debt   The Defendant, HENRY MARTIN, being arrested and failing to appear tho solemnly called, On motion of the Plantif by his Attorney, It is ordered that unless he appear at the next Court & answer this suit, Judgment be entered against him and ISRAEL SNEED & JAMES GAUNT, securities for his appearance for what shall appear due the Plantif & costs

    - The Same Plantif against JOSEPH DEGARNETT & NATHANIEL NORMENT Defts. In Debt   The Defendants being arrested & failing to appear tho solemnly called, On motion of the Plantif by his Attorney, It is ordered that unless the Defendants appear at the next Court & answer this suit, Judgment be entered against them & JOSEPH DEGARNETT JUNR., security for their appearance, for what shall appear due to the Plantif and costs

p   Caroline County Court 12th of June 1772
49   - JOHN GEORGE (Mill) Plantif against THOMAS BURK Defendt.   In Assault
    & Battery   Came the parties by their Attorneys and the Defendant prays leave til next Court to consider of & answer the Plantifs Writ & Declaration which is granted him

    - ROBERT GARROTT against THOMAS BUCKNER   In Debt
Dismissed, agreed

    - THOMAS HALEY Plantif against SAMUEL SALE   In Debt
The Defendant being arrest & failing to appear tho solemnly called, On motion of the Petitioner by his Attorney, It is ordered that unless the Defendant appear at the next Court & answer this suit, Judgment be entered against him & RICHARD JOHNSTON, security for his appearance, for what shall appear due to the Plantif & costs

    - GEORGE GUY Gent.,, Admor. of FARRELL & ANN HUGHES, Plt. against RICHARD JERVICE & FREDERICK FORTSON, Defendants   In Debt
The Defendants being arrested & failing to appear tho solemnly called, On motion of the Plantif by his Attorney, it is ordered that unless the Defendants appear at the next Court & answer this suit, Judgment be entered against them & JOHN GATEWOOD & THOMAS BURK, securities for their appearance, for what shall appear due to the Plantif & costs

    - WM: FLEET & BAYLOR WALKER, Exors. of JOHN SEMPLE deced., against JOHN GRIFFIN   On Petition   Came the parties by their Attorneys and on hearing the Testimony and arguments of both sides, it is considered by the Court that the Plantifs recover against the said Defendant Two pounds ten shillings current money. also their costs in this behalf expended; & the Defendant has leave til next Court to make appear any just discount before ROBERT GILCHRIST Gent.

p.   Caroline County Court 12th of June 1772
50   - WILLIAM FLEET & BAYLOR WALKER, Exors. of JOHN SEMPLE deced. against
        LAZALROUS YARBROUGH   On Petition   The Defendant being duly sum-
moned and failing to appear tho solemnly called, On motion of the Petitioners by their
Attorney, Judgment is granted them against the said Defendant for Two pounds eight
shillings & nine pence, the Debt in the Petition specified, also their costs in this behalf
expended
        - The Same against AMBROSE VAUGHN   On Petition
the Defendant being duly summoned and failing to appear tho solemnly called, On
motion of the Petitioners by their Attorney, Judgment is granted them against the said
Defendant for Three pounds nineteen shillings, the Debt in the Petition specified, also
their costs in this behalf expended, And the Petitioners acknowledged to have received
Two pounds seventeen shillings part thereof since the bringing this Petition
        - Ordered that the Court be adjourned til to morrow morning nine O'clock
The Minutes of the preceeding Orders were signed by
                                        EDMUND PENDLETON Gent.
(The remaining half of this page is blank.)

p.   At a Court continued and held for Caroline County the Fourteenth day of June
51   one thousand seven hundred and seventy two
                        Present his Majesties Justices
        EDMUND PENDLETON   WALKER TALIAFERRO &
        ROBERT GILCHRIST   JAMES MILLER   Gent.

        - Pursuant to an Order of Caroline Court, we of the Jury being first sworn have
caused an acre of Land belonging to JOHN BUCKNER, petitioned for by NICHOLAS WARE
to seventeen shillings & six pence, the damages accruing to the said JOHN BUCKNERs
land as the aforesaid acre to twenty two shillings and six pence and the damages
accruing to THOMAS BUCKNER by building the said Mill petitioned for by the said
NICHOLAS WARE to one pound fourteen shillings & two pence. Given under our hands &
seals the second day of June 1772. THOMAS SLAUGHTER, JOHN GARROTT, JAMES WARE,
JAMES MONDAY, JAMES PATTY, BENJAMIN ROBINSON, THOMAS SAMUEL, AMBROSE
DUDLEY. JOSEPH SAUNDERSON. DANIEL LAFOE, MOSES ROBINSON & JOHN JETER,. On
hearing the same, it is considered by the Court that the Petitioner be vested in the said
acre of land & leave is granted him on his paying the value thereof & the damages to
erect a Mill according to Law
        - WILLIAM FLEET & BAYLOR WALKER, Exors. of JOHN SEMPLE   against
FRANCIS STERN.   On Petition   Abates by return of the Sherif
        - The Same against JOHN REYNOLDS   On Petition   The same Order
        - The Same against WILLIAM PLUNKETT JUNR.   On Petition   The same Order
        - The Same against RICHARD DURRETT   On Petition   The same Order

p.   Caroline County Court 14th of June 1772
52   - WILLIAM FLEET & BAYLOR WALKER, Exors. of JOHN SEMPLE   against
        CHRISTOPHER SINGLETON.   On Petition   By Consent of parties by their
Attorneys, this suit is referred to the final determination of BENJAMIN HUBBARD Gent.
whose award is to be returned & make the Judgment of this Court
        - The Same against THOMAS REYNOLDS (Workman)   On Petition
The Defendant being duly summoned and failing to appear tho solemnly called, On
motion of the Petitioners by their Attorney, Judgment is granted them against the said

Defendant for one pound seven shillings & six pence, the Debt in the Petition, also their costs in this behalf expended

  - The Same against JOSEPH REYNOLDS On Petition

This suit abates by the Defendants death

  - The Same against WILLIAM REYNOLDS On Petition

The Defendant being duly summoned and failing to appear tho solemnly called, On motion of the Petitioners by their Attorney, Judgment is granted them against the said Defendant for three pounds seven shillings & six pence, the Debt in the Petition specified, also their costs in this behalf expended

  - The Same against EDWARD POWERS On Petition

Discontinued

  - The Same against CATHERINE LONG On Petition

The former summons in this suit not being executed, On motion of the Petitioners by their Attorney, a new summons is awarded them returnable to the next Court

  - The Same against BENJAMIN HOBBS & GEORGE MAJOR On Petition

Abates by Sherifs return as to HOBBS & dismissed as to MAJOR

p. <u>Caroline County Court 14th of June 1772</u>

53 - The Same against DANIEL LAFOE On Petition

  Came the parties by their Attorneys and the Court on hearing the Evidence & arguments of each party, do consider that the Petitioners recover against the said Defendant one pound seventeen shillings and three pence, also their costs in this behalf expended

  - The Same against AARON JERVICE On Petition

The Defendant being duly summoned and failing to appear tho solemnly called, On motion of the Petitioners by their Attorney, Judgment is granted them against the said Defendant for two pounds eighteen shillings & five pence, also their costs in this behalf expended

  - The Same against JAMES GAUNT On Petition

The Defendant being duly summoned and failing to appear tho solemnly called, On motion of the Petitioners by their Attorney, Judgment is granted them against the said Defendant for One pound fourteen shillings & six pence, the Debt in the Petition specified, also their costs in this behalf expended

  - The Same against JAMES GATEWOOD JUNR. On Petition

The Defendant being duly summoned and failing to appear tho solemnly called, On motion of the Petitioners by their Attorney, Judgment is granted against the said Defendant for three pounds thirteen shillings & three pence, the Debt in the Petition specified, also their costs in this behalf expended

  - the Same Plantifs against PHILLIP MAY Defendant In Case

  Came the parties by their Attorneys and the Defendant saving and reserving to himself all manner & advantage of exception as well to the Jurisdiction of the Court as to the Plantifs Writ and Declaration & prays leave til the next Court to consider of & answer thereto, which is granted him

p. <u>Caroline County Court 14th of June 1772</u>

54 - RICHARD JOHNSTON against DAVID & PEYTON STERNs On Petition

  The Defendants being duly summoned and failing to appear tho solemnly called On motion of the Petitioner by his Attorney, Judgment is granted him against the said Defendant for one pound fifteen shillings & eight pence seventy three pounds of nett tobacco & seven shillings & six pence, the Debt in the Petition specified, also his costs in this behalf expended

- PHILLIP JOHNSTON, Admor. of THOMAS JOHNSTON deceas'd against JAMES JOHNSON   In Case   By consent of the parties by their Attorneys, this suit is referred to the final determination of ROBERT GILCHRIST & JAMES MILLER. Gent., whose award is to be returned & made the Judgment of this Court

- EDWARD DIXON Gent., Plantif against PHILLIP JOHNSTON Defendt. In Case Came as well the Plantif by his Attorney as the Defendant in his own proper person & the said Defendant saith he cannot deny the Plantifs action so far as Five pounds two shillings and three pence; Therefore it is considered by the Court that the Plantif recover against the said Defendant the said sum of five pounds two shillings and three pence, the Debt by the Defendant in manner & form aforesaid confessed, also his costs in this bhealf expended, And the said Defendant in Mercy &c.

- JOHN TURNER Plt. against JOHN HARVEY Defendt.   In Case Came the parties by their Attorneys and the Defendant prays leave til the next Court to consider of and answer the Plantifs Writ & Declaration which is granted him

- GEORGE GAINES Plt. against WILLIAM REYNOLDS Deft. In Debt The former process in this suit not being executed, on the motion of the Plantif by his Attorney an alias is awarded him against the said Defendant returnable to the next Court

- WILLIAM SNODGRASS Plt. against HANNAH HERNDON, Exrs. of JAMES HERNDON deceased. Deft.   In Debt   Dismissed, agreed

pp   Caroline County Court 14th of June 1772
55   - RICHARD JOHNSTON, Exor. of FRANCIS COLEMAN, deced., against JEREMIAH PEIRCE   On Petition   Came the parties by their Attorney and on hearing the arguments & evidence of each party. it is considered by the Court that the same be dismissed & that the Defendant recover his costs in this behand expended

- EDWARD DIXON Gent., Plantif against JAMES CONDUIT Defendt.   In Case Came the parties by their Attorneys and the Defendant prays leave til the next Court to consider of & answer the Plantifs Writ & Declaration which is granted him

- The Same against JAMES CONDUIT, Admor. of THOMAS CONDUIT deced.
In Case   The same Order as last

- RICHARD JOHNSTON, Exr. of FRANCIS COLEMAN deced against JOHN GRIFFIN In Chancery   Came the parties by their Council and the Defendant prays leave til the next Court to consider of & answer the Plantiffs Bill which is granted him

- Messrs. DUNLOP & COMPY. against COSMO MEDICI   On Petition The Defendant being duly summoned and failing to appear tho solemnly called, On motion of the Petitioners by their Attorney, Judgment is granted them against the said Defendant for two pounds nine shillings & eleven pence, the Debt in the Petition specified. also their costs in this behalf expended

- JOHN GRAY & COMPY. Plantifs against THOMAS BURK Defendt. In Case The Defendant being arrested and failing to appear tho solemnly called, On motion of the Plantifs by their Attorney, It is ordered that unless the Defendant appear at the next Court and answer this suit. Judgment be entered against him and HENRY BURK, security for his appearance, which shall appear to be due the Plantifs & costs

p.   Caroline County Court 14th of June 1772
56   - JOHN PICKETT Plt against MILLY ASHBURN and JOHN DOWNER, Defendants
In Debt   Yesterday's Order set aside. Came the parties by their Attorneys and the Defendants relinquishing their plea acknowledge the Plantifs action, Therefore it is considered by the Court that the Plantif recover against the said Defendants

Eighty one pounds eight shillings, the Debt in the Declaration mentioned, also his costs
in this behalf expended, and the said Defendants in Mercy &c. This Judgment except the
costs is to be discharged by the payment of Forty pounds fourteen shillings current
money with legal Interest from the twenty first day of January one thousand seven
hundred and seventy one til paid; By Consent of the Plantif, the Defendants have leave
til the next Court to make any just discounts before WALKER TALIAFERRO Gent.
      - JOHN RICHARDS Plt. against JOHN RALLINS Defendt.   In Debt
The former Writ in this suit not being executed, On motion of the Plantif by his Attorney a new Writ is awarded him returnable to the next Court
      - EDWARD DIXON Plt. against EDMUND PENDLETON & JOSEPH ROBINSON Gent.,
Executors of BENJAMIN ROBINSON deced.   On a Writ of Scirefacias
Came the parties by their Attorneys and the Defendants relinquishing their plea,
acknowledge the Plantifs action, Therefore it is considered by the Court that the Plantif recover against the said Defendants Thirty two pounds one shillings & two pence,
One hundred & eighty two pounds of nett tobacco, the Debt in the said Writ specified,
also his costs in this behalf expended; And the said Defendants in Mercy &c.
      - JOHN HATLEY NOITON Plt. against JOHN ARMISTEAD Gent., Deft.   In Debt
Came the parties by their Attorneys and the Defendant relinquishing his plea acknowledges the Plantifs action, Therefore it is considered by the Court that the Plantif
recover against the said Defendant One hundred and Thirty pounds, Thirteen shillings
Sterling, the Debt in the Declaration mentioned, also his costs in this behalf expended
and the said

p   Caroline County Court 14th of June 1772
57   Defendant in Mercy &c., This Judgment except the costs is to be discharged by
         the payment of Sixty five pounds six shillings with legal Interest from the tenth
day of February one thousand seven hundred & Sixty nine til paid. This Debt & Interest
may be discharged in current money at 20 p cent difference of exchange
      - WILLIAM SMITH Plt. against WILLIAM SMITH Defendt.   In Debt
Came the Plantif by his Attorney and the Sherif having returned on an Attachment
awarded the Plantif in this suit that he had levied the same on an Ax, and the said Defendant being solemnly called & failed to appear and replevy the same, Therefore it is
considered by the Court that the Plantif recover against the said Defendant twelve
pounds nineteen shillings current money, the Debt in the Declaration mentioned, together with his costs by him in this behalf expended; And the said Defendant in Mercy &c.
This Judgment except the costs is to be discharged by the payment of six pounds nine
shillings & six pence with legal Interest from the Sixteenth day of October 1769 til paid,
By consent of the Plantif, it is ordered that the Sheriff release to the Defendant the
attached effects
      - LEONARD HARRISON Plt. against CHRISTOPHER SINGLETON Defendt. In Case
Came the parties by their Attorneys and the Defendant pleads Not Guilty, with leave,
which the Plantif joined and the trial thereof is referred til the next Court
      - DOCTOR WILLIAM JOHNSTON Plantif against ROBERT GILCHRIST Gent.,
Defendt.   In Case   Came the parties by their Attorneys & the Plantif prays leave til
the next Court to reply which is granted him
      -The Ch:Wdns. of Saint Margarets Parish against JOHN SUTTON   In Case
By consent of Parties by their Attorneys, JOHN MINOR & GEORGE GUY Gent. are added as
Referees in this suit

p.   Caroline County Court 14th day of June 1772
58   - WILLIAM DUDLEY Plt. against JOHN WILY Deft.   In Case
    This day came the parties by their Attorneys & the Defendant relinquishing his
plea acknowledges the Plantiffs action so far as to Nine pounds ten shillings & one
penny three farthings current money; It is Therefore considered by the Court that the
Plantif recover against the said Defendant the said sum, also his costs in this behalf
expended and the said Defendant in Mercy &c., By consent of the Plantif, the Defendt.
has leave til next Court to make out any just Discount before BENJAMIN HUBBARD Gent.
        - THOMAS SALE Plt. against SAMUEL SALE Deft.   In Trespass
Came the parties by their Attorneys and a Jury, to wit, ROBERT MICKLEBERRY foreman
&c., who being sworn well & truly to try the matter in issue joined, do say that the Defendant is Not Guilty of the Trespass in the Declaration charged; Therefore it is considered by the Court that the same be dismissed and that the Defendant recover against
the Plantif his costs by him in this behalf expended
        - WILLIAM BOWLER Plantif against JOHN SUTTON Defendt.   In Case
Came the parties by their Attorneys, & the Plantif prays further time til the next Court
to reply which is granted him
        - FRANCIS FLEMING Plantif against ANDREW HARRISON Defendt.   In Case
Came the parties by their Attorneys, & the Defendant pleads Not Guilty which the
Plantif joined & the trial thereof is referred til the next Court
        - The Same Plt. against The Same Deft.   In Case
The same Order as last
        - Ordered THOMAS SALE pay JOHN BRANSOME one hundred and twenty five
pounds of tobacco for attedning this Court five days as an evidence for him against
SAMUEL SALE
        - Ordered SAMUEL SALE pay WILLIAM HORD seventy five pounds of tobacco for
attending this Court three days as an evidence for him at the suit of THOS: SALE
        - Ordered SAMUEL SALE pay THOMAS HORD seventy five pounds of tobacco for
attending this Court three days as an evidence for him against SALE

p.   Caroline County Court 14th of June 1772
59   - JAMES MILLER Gent., Plantif   against   MORDECAI BUCKNER & OLIVER
        TOWLES Gent., Executors of LARKIN CHEW Gent., deceased
Pursuant to an award made & returned by JOSEPH JONES & JOHN SKINKER Gent., &
confessed by the Defendants to be just & right; It is considered by the Court that the
Plantif recover against the said Defendants Three hundred and sixty three pounds
eleven shillings and eleven pence with legal Interest from the twenty second day of
September one thousand seven hundred & Sixty seven til paid, also his costs in this
behalf expended. By consent of the Plantif, execution as to Two hundred pounds is to be
stayed til December next & for the residue til the 25th of September 1773
        - THOMAS PENNINGTON Plt. against ROBERT MONTH Deft.   In Debt
Came the parties by their Attorneys & the Defendant prays Oyer of the Writing Obligatory in the Declaration which is granted him
        - HENRY TERRILL against GARROTT HACKETT   On Petition
The Petitioner failing to prosecute this Petition, It is considered by the Court that the
same be dismissed. On motion of the Defendant by his Attorney, Judgment is granted
him against the Petitioner for his costs by him in this behalf expended
        - Present JOHN ARMISTEAD & WILLIAM BUCKNER, JUNR. Gent.
        - JAMES SHADDOCK against JOHN BARBY   In Case
The former process in this suit not being executed, On motion of the Plantif by his

Attorney, an Attachment is awarded him against the Estate of said Defendant & returnable to the next Court
        - RICHARD JERVICE Plt. against WILLIAM CHEWNING Deft.   In Case
The same order as last

p.   Caroline County Court 14th of June 1772
60   - The Justices Plts. against JAMES LOVERN &c. Defendts.   In Debt
        Came the parties by their Attorneys and the Defendants say that they have per-
formed the condition of their Bond; On motion of the Plantif time til the next Court is
granted him to reply
        - ROBERT FARGUSON Plt. against RICHARD & JAMES LOVERN Defts. In Case
 Came the parties by their Attorneys and the Defendants plead Non Assumpsit which
the Plantif joined and the trial thereof is referred til the next Court
        - JOHN CUMMIN Plt. against JAMES PATTIE Defendt.   )
        - The Same Plt. against The Same Defendt.   )
        - JAMES PATTIE Plt. against JOHN CUMMIN Defendt.   ) By consent of the
parties by their Attorneys, JAMES DUNLOP & ANDREW LECKIE Gent. are added as
Referees in this suit
        - BENJAMIN HUBBARD Gent. against JOSEPH PRICE   On Attachment
 The former Attachment not being executed, On motion of the Plantif by his Attorney a
new Attachment is awarded him against the Estate of the said Defendant returnable to
the next Court
        - JOHN CRAINE Plt. against JAMES GIMBOW Deft. The same Order as last
        - JOHN WALDEN against JOHN GOODRICH   On Petition
Came as well the Petitioner by his Attorney as the Defendant in his proper person &
the said Defendant saith he cannot deny the allegations in the Petition; Therefore it is
considered by the Court that the Plantif recover against the said Defendant Three
pounds currt. money, also his costs in this behalf expended; By consent of the Petitioner, the Deft. has leave to make appear any Discount before EUSIBIUS STONE Gent.

p.   Caroline County Court 14th of June 1772
61   - ROBERT SCOTT Plantif against WILLIAM GOODALL Deft.   In Debt
        Came the parties by their Attorneys and the Defendant relinquishing his plea
acknowledges the Plantifs action; Therefore it is considered by the Court that the
Plantif recover against the said Defendant Nine pounds ten shillings & ten pence with
legal Interest from the 20th day of January one thousand seven hundred and Seventy
one til paid, the Debt in the Declaration mentioned; together with his costs by him in
this behalf expended, And the said Defendant in Mercy &c.
        - GEORGE BULLARD Plt. against JOHN WILY Deft.   In Case
Discontinued
        - The Justices Plts. against WILLIAM BOWLER &c. Defts.   In Debt
Came the parties by their Attorneys & the Defendants pray time til the next Court to
rejoin which is granted them
        - HARRY BEVERLEY against EDWARD POWER   On Petition
This suit is dismissed at the costs of the Petitioner
        - WILLIAM BOWLER against LUNSFORD LOMAX   In Case
This suit abates by the Defendants death
        - JAMES WINSTON & JAMES OVERTON, Exors. of CHARLES GOODALL Gent. deceased
against WILLIAM BOWLER Deft.   On Writ of Scirefacias
Came the parties by their Attorneys and the Defendant relinquishing his plea ack-

nowledges the Plantifs action. Therefore it is considered by the Court that the Plantif recover against the said Defendant Fifty two pounds eight shillings. One hundred & nineteen pounds of nett tobacco & fifteen shillings or 150 lbs. of tobacco, the debt in the said Writ specified, together with their costs in this behalf expended. & the said Defendant in Mercy. &c., But this Judgment except the costs is to be discharged

p   Caroline County Court 14th of June 1772
62   by the payment of twenty six pounds four shillings currt. money with legal
        Interest from the nineteenth day of September 1764 til paid; One hundred and nineteen pounds of tobacco and fifteen shillings or 150 lbs. tobacco.
        - JAMES RITCHIE Esqr., & COMPY. Plts. against JOHN JESSE Defendt.   In Case
The Defendant being arrested & failing to appear tho solemnly called, On motion of the Plantifs by their Attorney, It is ordered that unless the Defendant appear at the next Court and answer the suit, Judgment will be entered against him & JAMES CAMPBELL, Security for his appearance, what shall appear due to the Plantifs & costs
        - FREDERICK FORTSON against JOHN WATKINS   On Attachment
The former Attachment not being executed, On motion of the Plantif, a new Attachment is awarded him against the Estate of the said Defendant returnable to the next Court
        - The Same against ISRAEL COGHILL   On Attachment
The same Order as last
        - ROBERT FLEMING BIBB against WILLIAM TIGNAL   On Debt
ROBERT FARISH & JOHN JOHNSTON Garnishees in this suit being duly summoned and failing to apear tho solemnly called. On motion of the Plantif by his Attorney an Attachment is awarded him against the said Defendant returnable to the next Court
        - HORATIO DADE Gent. Plt. against JOHN THILMAN Defendt.   In Case
Came as well the Plantif by his Attorney as the Defendant in his proper person and the said Defendant saith he cannot deny the Plantiffs action so far as to six pounds ten shillings current money. Therefore it is considered by the Court that the Plantif recover against the said Defendant the said sum of Six pounds ten shillings by the Defendant in manner & form aforesaid confessed, also his costs in this behalf expended; & by consent Execution on this Judgment is ordered to be stayed three months

p   Caroline County Court 14th of June 1772
63   - DAVID BOYD Gent. against JOHN GRIFFIN   On Petition
        The Defendant being duly summoned and failing to appear tho solemnly called, On motion of the Petitioner by his Attorney Judgment is granted him against the said Defendant for two pounds fourteen shillings & six pence, sixty pounds nett tobacco & seven shillings & six pence, the Debt in the Petition specified, also his costs in this behalf expended
        - GEORGE MAJOR Plantif against JOHN COOPER Defendt.   Assault & Battery
  The Defendant being arrested & failing to appear tho solemnly called, On motion of the Plantif by his Attorney, It is ordered that unless the Defendant appears at the next Court & answers this suit, Judgment will be entered against him for what shall appear due the Plantif & costs
        - ISAAC HAWES against RICHARD CONQUEST   On Petition
 The Defendant being duly summoned and failing to appear tho solemnly called, On motion of the Petitioner by his Attorney, Judgment is granted him against the said Defendant for Two pounds thirteen shillings & nine pence, the Debt in the Petition specified, also his costs in this behalf expended

- CATH. ROBERT & WM. REYNOLDS, Exrx. & Exr. of JAMES REYNOLDS deceased, against BENJAMIN HUBBARD & JOHN ELLIOT PAYNE   On Writ of Scirefacias
Came the parties by their Attorneys & the Defendants pray oyer of the said Writ & the Record therein mentioned which is granted them
   - JOHN GRAY & COMPY. Plts. against WM: WOODROOF Deft.   In Case
Abates by the Sheriffs return
   - The Same against JOHN MELEAR SENR.   On Petition
Abates by Defendants death

p   Caroline County Court 14th of June 1772
64   - EDWARD DIXON against WILLIAM BALLARD JUNR.   On Petition
   The Defendant being duly summoned and failing to appear tho solemnly called, On motion of the Petitioner by his Attorney, Judgment is granted him against the said Defendant for Two pounds eighteen shillings & ten pence, the Debt in the Petition specified. also his costs in this behalf expended
   - EDWARD DIXON against WILLIAM LOYDE   On Petition
The Defendant being duly summoned and failing to appear tho solemnly called. On motion of the Petitioner by his Attorney, Judgment is granted him against the said Defendant for four pounds one shilling & three pence, the Debt in the Petition specified, also his costs in this behalf expended
   - EDWARD DIXON against JOHN MELEAR SENR.   On Petition
Abates by Defendants death
   - JOHN GRAY & COMPY. Plts. against JOHN GOODRICH Deft.   In Debt
JOHN ARMISTEAD Gent., entered himself Special Bail for the Defendant according to Law
   - The Same Plts. against The Same Deft.   In Case
JOHN ARMISTEAD Gent. entered himself Special Bail for the Defendant according to Law
   - EDWARD DIXON Gent., Plt. against JOHN MELEAR JUNR In Case
The Defendant being arrested and failing to appear tho solemnly called. On motion of the Plantif by his Attorney. It is ordered that unless the Defendant appear at the next Court & answer the suit, Judgment will be entered against him and WILLIAM TOOMBS, Security for his appearance. for what shall appear due the Plantif & costs
   - JOHN SEMPLE deced.. Exors. against JOHN ROYSTON   On Petition
Dismissed

p   Caroline County Court 14th of June 1772
65   JOHN GRAY & COMPY. Plts. against JOHN GOODRICH Defendt.   In Debt
JOHN ARMISTEAD Gent., in discharge of his recognizance delivered the Defendant up in Court and the said Defendant saith he cannot deny the Plantiffs action. On Motion of the Plantif by his Attorney. It is considered by the Court that the Plantif recover against the said Defendant. Thirty eight pounds nineteen shillings. the Debt in the Declaration mentioned; also his costs in this behalf expended; And the said Defendant in Mercy &c.. But this Judgment except the costs is to be discharged by the payment of Nineteen pounds nine shillings & six pence with legal Interest from the second day of August one thousand seven hundred & seventy til paid
   - JOHN GRAY & COMPY Plts. against JOHN GOODRICH Defendt. In Case
JOHN ARMISTEAD Gent.. in discharge of his recognizance delivered the Defendant up in Court and the said Defendant saith he cannot deny the Plantifs action so far as to Six pounds nine shillgs. & eight pence currt. money; On motion of the Plantif by his Attor-

ney. it is considered by the Court that they recover against the said Defendant the said sum of six pounds nine shillings & eight pence by the Defendant in manner & form aforesaid confessed, together with their costs in this behalf expended, And the said Defendant in Mercy &c

  - EDWARD DIXON Plt. againt WILLIAM TOOMBS Deft. In Case
The Defendant being arrested & failing to appear tho solemnly called, On motion of the Plantif by his Attorney, It is ordered that unless the Defendant appear at the next Court and answer this suit. Judgment be entered against him & WILLIAM TOOMBS, Security for his appearance, for what shall appear to be due & costs

  - WILLIAM FLEET & BAYLOR WALKER Exrs. of JOHN SEMPLE deced., against WILLIAM WHITLOCE   Dismissed

p. Caroline County Court 14th of June 1772
66 - WILLIAM & MARY BROWN, Exr. & Exrx. of JOHN BROWN deced., against
  JOHN THILMAN Defendant In Debt The Defendant being arrested & failing to appear tho solemnly called, On motion of the Plantif by his Attorney, It is ordered that unless the Defendant appear at the next Court & answer this suit, Judgment be entered against him and JAMES HEAD LYNCH, Security for his appearance, for what shall appear due the Plantif & costs

  - JACOB (? CLININGHOLTZ) assignee of THOMAS NORMENT against MILES CANBY & JOHN GEORGE Defts. In Debt JOHN PENN Gent., entered himself Special Bail for the Defendants according to Law; The came the parties by their Attorneys and JOHN GEORGE saving & reserving to himself all advantage of Exception as well to the Jurisdiction of the Court as to the Plantifs Writ & Declaration & prays time til the next Court to consider of & answer thereto, which is granted him. And the suit abates as to the Defendant. MILES CANBY, by the Sheriffs return

  - ANDREW COCHRAN & COMPY. against JOSEPH DEGARNETT On Writ of Scirefacias Came the parties by their Attorneys & the Defendant prays oyer of the said Writ & the Record therein mentioned which is granted him

  - BARTELET ANDERSON, Exr. of HARRY ROBINSON Plt. against ROBERT WOOLFOLK JUNR. On Petition The Defendant being duly summoned & failing to appear tho solemnly called, On motion of the Petitioner by his Attorney, Judgment is granted him against the said Defendant for Two pounds eight shillings & one penny half penny with legal Interest from the Twelvth day of September 1771 til paid, the Debt in the Petition specified; also his costs in this behalf expended

  - LODOWICH JONES MAJOR Plt. against BENJAMIN ALSOP Deft. In Assault & Battery Came the parties by their Attorneys, & the Defendant prays time til next Court to consider of & anser the Plantifs Writ & Declaration which is granted him

p. Caroline County Court 14th of June 1772
67 - JOSEPH SMITH Plt against RICHARD PHILLIPS & WILLIAM CARTER Defts.
  In Debt Discontinuance against PHILLIPS & the former process not being executed, On motion of the Plantif by his Attorney, an Attachment is awarded him against the Estate of the said Defendant returnable to the next Court

  - ROBERT SMITH Plt. against WILLIAM PETTIS Deft. In Debt
JOSEPH RICHESON Special Bail for the Defendant according to Law, & came the parties by their Attorneys & the Defendant prays oyer of the Writing Obligatory in the declaration mentioned which is granted him

  - ROBERT SMITH Plt against EDWARD HUNT, EDWARD BOWCOCK & JOHN RAGAN Defendts. In Debt   This suit abates as to BOWCOCK by return & JOHN JONES Special Bail for the other Defendants according to Law, & came the said parties by their Attorneys & the Defendants pray oyer of the Writing Obligatory in the Declaration mentioned which is granted them

 - BENJAMIN ELLIOTT & LISTON TEMPLE Plts. against JOHN FARGUSON Defendant   In Debt   The former Writ in this suit not being executed, On motion of the Plantifs by their Attorney, a new Writ is awarded them returnable to the next Court

 - RICHARD GOODALL Plt. against ROBERT MICKLEBERRY Deft.   In Case By consent of parties by their Attorneys, this suit is referred to the final determination of THOMAS CLAIBORNE, JOHN PENN & EDMUND PENDLETON JUNR., Gent., whose awards is to be returned & made the Judgment of this Court

 - THOMAS BELL against CHRISTOPHER SINGLETON   On Petition Came the parties by their Attorneys and the Court on hearing the Testimony & arguments of each party, do consider that the

p   Caroline County Court 14th of June 1772
68   Petitioner recover against the said Defendant Two pounds fifteen shillings, also his costs in this behalf expended

 - JOHN SUTTON Plt. against ROBERT WOOLFOLK, Defendt.   In Debt The Defendant being arrested & failing to appear tho solemnly called, On motion of the Plantif by his Attorney, It is ordered that unless the Defendant appear at the next Court and answer this suit, Judgment be entered against him and JOHN THILMAN, Security for his appearance, for what shall appear due to the Plantif & costs

 - Ordered THOMAS BELL pay WILLIAM LOYD one hundred and fifty pounds of tobacco for attending this Court six days as an evidence for him against SINGLETON

 - JOHN TAYLOR & JOHN PENN Gent. against WILLIAM BROWN SENR.   On Petition The Defendant being duly summoned & failing to appear tho solemnly called, On motion of the Petitioners by their Attorney, Judgment is granted against the said Defendant for two pounds seven shillings & nine pence, the Debt in the Petition specified, also their costs in this behalf expended

 - The Same against THOMAS BROWN   On Petition The Defendant being duly summoned & failing to appear tho solemnly called, On motion of the Petitioners by their Attorney, Judgment is granted them against the said Defendant for two pounds thirteen shillings & one penny, the Debt in the Petition specified, also their costs in this behalf expended

 - The Same against THOMAS TARRANT   On Petition The Defendant being duly summoned & failing to appear tho solemnly called, On motion of the Petitioners by their Attorney, Judgment is granted them against the said Defendant for three pounds six shillings & elevenpence half penny, the Debt in the Petition specified, also their costs in this behalf expended

 - ROBERT GILCHRIST Gent., against PATRICK CARY   On Petition Abates by the return of the Sheriff

p   Caroline County Court 14th of June 1772
69   - JAMES BOWIE JUNR. Plt. against JOHN BILLOPS Defendt.   In Case The Defendant being arrested & failing to appear tho solemnly called, On motion of the Plantif by his Attorney, It is ordered that unless the Defendant appear at the next Court & answer this suit, Judgment will be entered against him and HENRY PEMBERTON, security for his appearance, for what shall be due the Plantif & costs

 - ROBERT GILCHRIST Gent., Plt. against ELIJAH DANIEL Defendt.   In Case The former Writ in this suit not being executed, On motion of the Plantif by his Attor-

ney. It is ordered that unless the Defendant appear at the next Court & answer this suit,
Judgment be entered against him for what shall appear to be due the Plantif & costs
        - The Same Plt. against REUBIN ROYSTON Deft.   In Case
The former Writ in this suit not being executed, On motion of the Plantif by his
Attorney a new Writ is awarded him returnable to the next Court
        - The Same Plt. against ELLIOT EMMERSON & PATTY his Wife   On Petition
The Defendants being duly summoned & failing to appear tho solemnly called, On
motion of the Petitioner by his Attorney, Judgment is granted him against the said
Defendnat for Five pounds, the Debt in the Petition specified, also his costs in this be-
half expended
        - MILCHE. BRAIME & RICHARD WYAT, Exors. of WALTER CHILES deced., against
ROBERT WOOLFOLK & JAMES BABER   In Debt   The Defendants being
arrested & failing to appear tho solemnly called, On motion of the Plantifs by their
Attorney It is ordered

p   Caroline County Court 14th of June 1772
70   that unless the Defendants appear at the next Court & answer this suit, Judgment
         be entered against them & JOHN GEORGE & JAS: ISBELL, security for their
appearance for what shall appear to be due the Plantifs & costs
        - The Same Plts. against WILLIAM BROWN & JOHN THILMAN Defts. In Debt
The process in this suit not being executed, On the motion of the Plantifs by their
Attorney, an Attachment is awarded them against the Estate of the said Defendant returnable to the next Court, & the Defendant, THILMAN, being arrested & failing to
appear tho solemnly called, It is ordered that unless the Defendant appear at the next
Court & answer this suit, Judgment be entered against him and JAMES HEAD LYNCH,
security for his appearance, for what shall appear due the Plantifs & costs
        - WILLIAM CHILES & MELCHISEDECK BRAIME, Exors. of WALTER CHILES deceased
against   JAMES HEAD LYNCH & BENJAMIN JOHNSON Defts. In Debt
The Defendants being duly arrested & failing to appear tho solemnly called, On motion
of the Plantifs by their Attorney, It is ordered that unless the Defendants appear at the
next Court and answer this suit, Judgment be entered against them and JOHN THILMAN,
Security for their appearance, for what shall appear to be due the Plantifs & costs
        - WILLIAM MONTGOMERY & Son against ANTHONY LAFON On Writ of Scire-
facias   The former Writ in this suit not being executed, On motion of the Plantifs by
their Attorney, a new Writ is awarded them returnable to the next Court
        - EDWARD DIXON Plantif, against JAMES FLETCHER Defendt.   In Trespass
Came the parties by their Attorney & the Defendant prays time til next Court to
consider of & answer the Plantifs Writ & Declaration, which is granted him
        - THOMAS BURK Plt. against JOHN GRUMBLEY Deft.,   In Case
Dismissed, agreed

p   . Caroline County Court 14th of June 1772
71   - PARK GOODALL Quitam Plt. against GARROTT HACKETT Defendt. In Debt
         Came the parties by their Attorneys & the Defendant saving & reserving to him-
self all advantage of exception as well to the Jurisdiction of the Court as to the Plantifs
Writ & Declaration, & prays time til next Court to consider of & answer thereto, which is
granted him
        - JACOB BURRUS & JOHN THOMPSON Plts. against JOHN THILMAN Defendt.
In Debt   The former Writ in this suit not being executed, On motion of the
Plantiffs by their Attorney, a new Writ is awarded them returnable to the next Court

- The Executors of PHILLIP GRYMES Gent., deced., Complts. against
LUNSFORD LOMAX Defendt.   In Ejectment.   Abates by the Defendants death
- ROBERT GARROTT Plt. against MARGARET KENNOR, Exrx. of GEORGE KENNOR
deced. Deft., In Case   Came the parties by their Attorneys & the Defendant pleads
Non Assumpsit, which the Plantif joined & the trial thereof is referred til next Court
- JOHN HEWETT Plantif against JOHN PENN Defendt.   In Case
Came the parties by their Attorneys & the Defendant prays further time til next Court
to consider of & answer the Plantifs Writ & Declaration which is granted him
- RICHARD SEAGOR Plantif against HENRY DURRETT & JOHN DURRETT Defts.
In Debt   Came the parties by their Attorneys & the Defendants relinquishing their
plea acknowledge the Plantifs action; Therefore it is considered by the Court that the
Plantif recover against the said Defendants One hundred & one pounds five shillings
the Debt in the Declaration mentioned together with his costs by him in this behalf
expended; And the said Defendants in Mercy, &c., This Judgment except the costs is to be
discharged by the payment of fifty pounds twelve shillings & six pence with legal Interest from the fifteenth day of December 1770 til paid

p   Caroline County Court 14th of June 1772
72   - WILLIAM FLEET & BAYLOR WALKER, Exors of JOHN SEMPLE deced., against
           LUNSFORD LOMAX   In Case   This suit abates by the Defendants death
           - GEORGE LUMSDEN against WILLIAM HACKNEY   On Petition
The parties by their Attorneys & on hearing the Testimony and Arguments of both
sides. It is considered by the Court that the Petitioner recover against the said Defendant One pound ten shillgs. and three pence, the Debt in the Petition specified together
with his costs by him in this behalf expended
           - JAMES SACREY Plantif against AMBROSE JETER Defendt.   In Case
Came the parties by their Attorneys, & the Defendant pleads Not Guilty with leave.
which the Plantif joined & the trial thereof is referred til the next Court
           - The Same Plt. against ROY GRIFFIN Deft.   In Case
The same Order as last
           - DAVID STERN Plt. against WILLIAM FOX   In Case
Came the parties by their Attorneys & the Defendant prays further time til the next
Court to consider of & answer the Plantifs Writ & Declaration which is granted him
           - WILLIAM PEMBERTON, Assignee of THOMAS BERRY & CORNELIUS VAUGHN,
Plantifs against JOSEPH DEGARNETT & NATHANIEL NORMENT, Defts.   In Debt
The former Writ not being executed on the Defendant, DEGARNETT, On motion of the
Plantif by his Attorney, an Attachment is awarded him against the Estate of the said
Defendant returnable to the next Court & the Defendant, NORMENT, being arrest &
failing to appear tho: solemnly called, It is ordered that unless the Defendant appear at
the next Court and answer this suit, Judgment be entered against him & JOHN TURNER
JUNR. Security for his appearance, for what shall appear due to the Plts. & costs

p.   Caroline County Court 14th of June 1772
73   - HENRY WINSLOW Plt. against GARROTT HACKETT Deft.   In Case
           The Defendant being arrested & failing to appear tho: solemnly called, On
motion of the Plantif by his Attorney, It is ordered that unless the Defendant appear at
the next Court & answer this suit, Judgment be entered against him & RICHARD ROY,
security for his appearance, for what shall appear due the Plantif and costs
           - WILLIAM ABBOTT against ANN MITCHELL   On Petition
The Defendant being duly summoned & failing to appear tho: solemnly called, On

motion of the Petitioner by his Attorney, Judgment is granted him against the said Defendant for One pound seven shillings & six pence the Debt in the Petition specified, also his costs in this behalf expended

    - HOLT RICHESON, Admr. of CHS: SEATON against JOHN SUTTON   In Case
By consent of parties by their Attorneys, this suit is referred to the final determination of EDMUND PENDLETON, Gent., whose award is to be returned & made the Judgment of this Court

    - CHARLES GORDON, Assignee of JOHN GAINES, who was Assignee of JOHN TALBERT against BENJAMIN JOHNSTON   In Debt   Abates by the Sheriffs return

    - CHARLES SEATON Admor. against ACHILLIS WHITLOCK   On Writ of Scirefacias
The former Writ in this suit not being executed, On motion of the Plantif by his Attorney, It is ordered that a new Writ issue returnable to the next Court

    - GEORGE GUY Admor. of FARRELL & ANN HUGHES, deced. Plt. against FREDERICK FORTSON & THOMAS BURK   Defendts.   In Debt
The Defendants being arrested & failing to appear tho: solemnly called, On motion of the Plantif by his Attorney, It is ordered that unless

p   Caroline County Court 14th of June 1772
74   the Defendants appear at the next Court & answer this suit, Judgment be entered against them & JOHN ALEXANDER STILL, security for their appearance, for what shall appear due to the Plts. & costs

    - WILLIAM FLEET & BAYLOR WALKER, Exors. of JOHN SEMPLE deceased, Plts. against HARRY BEVERLEY Defendt.   In Case   Came the parties by their Attorneys, & the Jury. to wit, SAMUEL MAJOR foreman &c., who being impanelled & sworn well & truly to enquire the damages in this suit, do say that the Plantifs have sustained damage by reason of the said Defendant to Thirty four pounds ten shillings current money, Therefore it is considered by the Court that the Plantifs recover against the said Defendant & JAMES TAYLOR Gent. Sherif, his damages aforesaid by the Jurors in form aforesaid assessed, together with their costs in this behalf expended & the said Defendant in Mercy &c.

    - McCALL & SHEDDEN against HENRY MARTIN   On Petition
The Defendant being duly summoned and failing to appear tho: solemnly called, On motion of the Petitioner by their Attorney, Judgment is granted them against the said Defendant for four pounds thirteen shillings & one penny, the Debt in the Petition specified. also their costs in this behalf expended

    - JOHN TAYLOR & JOHN PENN Gent., Plts. against HUMPHREY HALEY Deft.
In Debt.   The Defendant being arrested & failing to appear tho: solemnly called, On motion of the Plantiffs by their Attorney, It is ordered that unless the Defendant appear at the next Court & answer this suit, Judgment will be entered against him and RICHARD GEORGE, security for his appearance, for what shall appear to be due the Plts. & costs

    - The Same Plts. against WILLIAM MEATCHEM Deft.   In Debt
The Process in this suit not being executed, On motion of the Plantifs by their Attorney an Attachment is awarded them against the said Defendt. returnable to the next Court

    - The Same Plts. against STEPHEN FORTSON Deft.   In Debt
The same Order as last

p.   Caroline County Court 14th of June 1772
75   - JOHN TAYLOR & JOHN PENN Gent. Plantiffs against JOHN GEORGE Defendt.
In Debt   ROBERT MICKLEBERRY Special Bail for the Defendant according to Law. Then came the parties by their Attorneys & the Defendant prays oyer of the Writing Obligatory in the Declaration mentioned, which is granted him

- JOHN TAYLOR & JOHN PENN Gent. Plts. against WILLIAM SOUTHWORTH
Deft.   In Debt   On motion of the Plantifs by their Attorney, Judgment is granted
them against the said Defendant for their costs by them in this behalf expended
        - The Same Plts against WILLIAM SOUTHWORTH JUNR., Deft.   In Debt
The Defendant being arrested & failing to appear tho: solemnly called, On motion of
the Plantifs by their Attorney, It is ordered that unless the Defendant appear at the
next Court & answer this suit, Judgment be entered against him & JOHN GEORGE, (Hhd)
Security for his appearance, for what shall appear due the Plantifs & costs
        - The Same Plts. against REUBIN HERNDON Defendt.   In Debt
Came the Plantifs as well by their Attorney as the Defendant in his proper person &
the said Defendant agrees that Judgment should be entered against him according to
Bond, It is therefore considered by the Court that the Plantifs recover against the said
Defendant Twenty six pounds currt. money, the Debt in the Declaration mentioned, together with his costs in this behalf expended; & the said Defendant in Mercy &c., But
this Judgment except the costs is to be discharged by the payment of Thirteen pounds
with legal Interest from the twenty sixth day of December 1771 til paid
        - The Same Plts. against JOHN HARVEY   Defendt.   In Debt
WILLIAM WHITLOCK entered himself Special Bail for the Defendant according to Law,
& came the parties by their Attorneys & the Defendant prays Oyer of the Writing Obligatory in the Declaration mentioned which is granted him

p.   Caroline County Court 14th of June 1772
76   - JOHN TAYLOR & JOHN PENN Gent., Plts. against THOMAS ALLEN Defendt.
        In Debt   The former Writ in this suit not being executed, On motion of the
Plantifs by their Attorney, a new Writ is awarded them returnable to the next Court
        - The Same against BENJAMIN GRAVES   On Petition
The Defendant being duly summoned & failing to appear tho: solemnly called, On
motion of the Petitioners by their Attorney, It is considered by the Court that they recover against the said Defendant one pound five shillings & two pence, the Debt in the
Petition specified, also their costs in this behalf expended
        - The Same against BENJAMIN MILWARD   On Petition
The Defendant being duly summoned & failing to appear tho: solemnly called, On
motion of the Petitioners by their Attorney, Judgment is granted them against the said
Defendant for four pounds four shillings & three pence, the Debt in the Petition specified, also their costs in this behalf expended, But this Judgment except the costs is to be
discharged by the payment of Two pounds two shillings and one penny half penny
with legal Interest from the 18th dy of December one thousand seven hundred &
seventy one til paid
        - The Same Plts. against JOHN SMITH Defendt.   In Debt
Came as well the Plantifs by their Attorney as the Defendant in his proper person &
the said Defendant saith that he agrees that Judgment should be entered against him
according to Bond; Therefore it is considered by the Court that the Plantifs recover
against the Defendant Eleven pounds sixteen shillings, the Debt in the Declaration
mentioned, also their costs in this behalf expended; But this Judgment except the costs
is to be discharged by the payment of five pounds eighteen shillings with legal Interest
from the 21st day of December one thousand seven hundred & seventy one til paid. By
consent, Execution on this Judgment is ordered to be stayed three months
        - The Same Plts. against THOMAS JERVICE Deft.   In Debt
The Defendant being arrested & failing to appear tho: solemnly called, On motion of
the Plantifs by their Attorney, It is ordered that

p.   Caroline County Court 14th of June 1772
77   unless the Defendant appears at the next Court & answers this suit, Judgment
      will be entered against him & RICHARD GEORGE, security for his appearance, for
what shall appear to e due the Plantifs & costs
      - JOHN TAYLOR & JOHN PENN, Gent. against BARTHOLOMEW CHEWNING
   On Petition   The Defendant being duly summoned and failing to appear tho: solemnly
called. On motion of the Petitioners by their Attorney, Judgment is granted them
against the said Defendant for three pounds fifteen shillings & four pence, the Debt in
the Petition specified, also their costs in this behalf expended; But this Judgment except
the costs is to be discharged by the payment of One pound seventeen shillings & eight
pence with legal Interest from the 16th day of December one thousand seven hundred
& seventy one til paid
      - The Same Plts. against JAMES YARBROUGH Defendt.   In Debt
   The Defendant being arrested & failing to appear tho: solemnly called, On motion of
the Plantiffs by their Attorney, It is ordered that unless the Defendant appear at the
next Court & answer this suit, Judgment will be entered against him & JOHN GEORGE
(Hhd) security for his appearance, for what shall appear to be due the Plantifs & costs
      - The Same Plts. against WILLIAM MADDISON Defendt.   In Case
   The Defendant being arrested & failing to appear tho: solemnly called, On motion of
the Plantiffs by their Attorney, It is ordered that unless the Defendant appear at the
next Court & answer this suit, Judgment be entered against him & WILLIAM QUARLES,
security for his appearance, for what shall appear due the Plantifs & costs
      - The Same Plts. against CHRISTOPHER ROBINSON Deft.   In Chancery
   Came the Complainants by their Council and the Defendant by a Note from under his
hand agrees that a Decree may be entered against him for Seven pounds six shillings &
nine pence with legal Interest, staying execution thereof til October next; Therefore it
is considered by the Court and is decreed & ordered, that the Complainants recover
against the said Deft., the said sum of Seven pounds six shillings & nine pence with
legal Interest from the sixth day of November one thousand seven hundred and

p   Caroline County Court 14th of June 1772
78   seventy one til paid, also their costs in this behalf expended; And it is also
     decreed & ordered that unless the Defendant shall satisfy the Complainants their
Debt and costs on or before the first day of October next, he be foreclosed of all Equity of
Redemption in the Mortgaged premises in the Bill mentioned, And that the Complts. be
at liberty to sell & dispose of the same on Credit til April next
      - JOHN TAYLOR & JOHN PENN Complts. against LODOWICH GEORGE Defendt.
   In Chancery   Came the Complainants by their Council & the Defendant being sum-
moned & failing to appear & answer this suit, an Attachment is awarded agains the said
Defendant returnable to the next Court.
      - An Inventory & Appraisement of the Estate of THOMAS JOHNSTON deceased
returned & ordered to be recorded
      - JOHN MELEAR JUNR. Plantif against RICHARD GOODALL Defendt.   In Debt
   The Plantif failing to appear & prosecute this suit, On motion of the Defendant by his
Attorney, Judgment is granted him against the Plantif for his costs by him in this
behalf expended
      - RICHARD GOODALL against JOHN MELEAR JUNR.   On Petition
Dismissed

- EDWARD DIXON & JOHN SKINKER, Gent., Exors. of THOMAS TURNER deced., Plts, against NATHANIEL BURWELL & JOHN ARMISTEAD Gent. Acting Executors of JOHN BAYLOR Esqr. deced., Defts.   In Debt   Came as well the Plantifs by their Attorneys as the Defendants and the Defendants agree that Judgment should be entered against them according to Bond; Therefore it is considered by the Court that the Plantifs recover against the said Defendants, Four hundred pounds current money, the Debt in the Declaration mentioned; also their costs in this behalf expended, & this Judgment except the costs is to be discharged by the payment of Twelve pounds seventeen shillings & eleven pence current money with legal Interest from the seventh day of March one thousand seven hundred and seventy one til paid. By Consent Execution on this Judgment is stayed til October next

p.   **Caroline County Court 14th of June 1772**
79   - MUSCOE GARNETT,Executor of JAMES GARNETT, against SAMUEL MAJOR
On Petition   The Defendant being duly summoned and failing to appear tho: solemnly called, On motion of the Petitioner by his Attorney, Judgment is granted him against the said Defendant for Five pounds current money, the Debt in the Petition specified; also his costs in this behalf expended
     - EDWARD DIXON, Assignee of ANTHY: THORNTON, Gt., Plt., against CHARLES ROBINSON & CHARLES CARTER, Admors. of BEN: ROBINSON JUNR.   In Debt
Came the parties by their Attorney & the Defendants pray Oyer of the Writing Obligatory in the Declaration mentioned which is granted them
     - The Same Plt. against THOMAS SLAUGHTER Defendt.   In Debt
The same Order as last
     - ANDREW THOMPSON & COMPY. Plts. against JOHN (too faded) Defendant
In Debt   The same Order as last
     - The Same Plts. against JOHN SULLENGER Defendt.   In Debt
Dismissed by consent of parties
     - ROBERT (faded) Plt. against YOUNGER PITTS, Exor. of WILLIAM PITTS
Defendant   In Case   Came the parties by their Attorneys and the Defendant saving & reserving all advantage of exception as well to the Jurisdiction of the Court as well as the Plantifs Writ & Declaration, prays leave til the next Court to consider of & answer thereto which is granted him
     - JOHN KINSEY Plt. against RICHARD JOHNSON, Exor. of FRANCIS COLEMAN deced., Deft.,   In Case   The same Order as last
     - GEORGE RIPPEN & COMPY. Plts. against JAMES PITTS, Defendt.   In Case
Came the Plantifs by their Attorney, On his motion the former Writ in this suit not being executed, a new Writ is awarded them returnable to the next Court

p.   **Caroline County Court 14th of June 1772**
80   - For reasons appearing to the Court, (   ) THORNTON Gent. is excused from the Presentment the Grand Jury found against him for not keeping his Road in Repair according to Law
     - HENRY LYNE JUNR. against ROBERT WOOLFOLK JUNR.   On Petition
The Defendant being duly summoned & failing to appear tho: solemnly called, On motion of the Petitioner by his Attorney, Judgment is granted him against the said Defendant for Two pounds seven shillings and six pence with legal Interest from the Tenth day of December one thousand seven hundred & seventy one til paid; also his costs in this behalf expended

- PHILLIP MOUNTAGUE, Exor. of WILLIAM ROANE deced., against DANIEL HAYS
On Petition   The Defendant being duly summoned and failing to appear tho: solemnly
called, On motion of the Petitioner by his Attorney, Judgment is granted him against
the said Defendant for Four pounds the Debt in the Petition specified, also his costs in
this behalf expended

- ANDREW THOMPSON & COMPY. Plts. against WILLIAM HILTON Defendant
In Debt   Came as well the Plantifs by their Attorney as the Defendant by Note from
his under his hand agrees that Judgment should be entered against him according to
Bond; Therefore it is considered by the Court that the Plantifs recover against the said
Defendant One hundred & twenty six pounds one shilling, the Debt in the Declaration
mentioned; also their costs in this behalf expended; But this Judgment, except the costs,
is to be discharged by the payment of Eighty eight pounds & six pence current money
with legal Interest from the sixth day of April one thousand seven hundred & seventy
one til paid; By Consent of the Plantifs, execution on this Judgment is stayed til the first
of September 1772

- The Executors of JAMES REYNOLDS deced., Plts. against ROBERT GILCHRIST
Gent., Exor. of JOHN MILLER deced., Deft.   In Case
Came the parties by their Attorneys & the Defendant prays leave til the next Court to
consider of & answer the Plantifs Writ & Declaration which is granted him

p.   Caroline County Court 14th of June 1772
81   - BENJAMIN ROBINSON, an Infant, by JOSEPH ROBINSON his next Friend
          against ROBERT PARKER   Assault & Battery   The Defendant being
arrested & failing to appear tho: solemnly called, On motion of the Plantif by his Attorney, it is ordered that unless the Defendant appear at the next Court & answer this suit,
Judgment be entered against him for what shall appear to be due the Plantif & costs

- Our Sovereign Lord the King   against   FREDERICK & STEPHEN FORTSON,
MICHL. DONOHOE & ROBERT WOOLFOLK   Grand Jury Presentments
The former summons not being executed, On motion of the Plantif by his Attorney, a
new summons is awarded him returnable to the next Court

- LAWRENCE TALIAFERRO against JOHN MILLER Gent.   In Ejectment
Came the parties by their Attorneys, & on motion of the Plantif a new Survey is
awarded him & It is ordered that ROBERT GILCHRIST, WILLIAM WOODFORD & JOHN
BUCKNER & THOMAS LOWRY Gent., or any two of them, attend the Survey & Sheriff
while they are making the Survey

- Ordered that the Court be adjourned til the Court in Course
- The Minutes of the preceeding Orders were signed by
                                        EDMUND PENDLETON, Gent.

p.   At a Court held for Caroline County the Ninth day of July One thousand seven
82   hundred & seventy two
          By Virtue of a Commission from under the hand of his Excellency the Governour
& Seal of the Colony, which being read as usual, ROBERT GILCHRIST & JAMES TAYLOR
Gent., administered the Oaths to his Majestys person & Government to EDMUND PENDLE-
TON, Gent., who repeated and subscribed the Test & took the Oath of a Justice of the Peace
in Common Law, Chancery & Oyer & Terminer, and then the said EDMUND PENDLETON
administered the said Oaths to his Majestys person and Government to ROBERT GIL-
CHRIST, JAMES MILLER, WILLIAM WOODFORD, JOHN BUCKNER, JOHN ARMISTEAD, WIL-
LIAM BUCKNER JUNR., SAMUEL HAWES, JAMES UPSHAW, GAWIN CORBIN, ROGER
QUARLES & GEORGE GUY Gent., who repeated & subscribed the Test & took the Oath of a
Justice of the Peace in Common Law, Chancery & Oyer & Terminer

Present His Majestys Justices
EDMUND PENDLETON   WILLIAM BUCKNER
JAMES TAYLOR   JAMES UPSHAW
WALKER TALIAFERRO   and   Gent.
WILLIAM WOODFORD   GEORGE GUY

- FREDERICK FORTSON Plantif against JAMES GREGORY Defendt. Assault &
Battery   Dismissed, agreed
- An Inventory & Appraisement of the Estate of SARAH FARISH returned and
ordered to be recorded
- JOHN GRAY & COMPY. Plts. gainst RICHARD WOOLFOLK, ROBERT WOOLFOLK,
& PAUL THILMAN Defts.   In Debt   On motion of the Plantiffs by their Attor-
ney, Judgment is granted them against the said Defendants for their costs in this behalf
expended
- Ordered JAMES TAYLOR Gent., Treasurer of this County, pay GEORGE YATES
Twenty pounds currt. money for repairing the Causeway at GUINEAS BRIDGES if suf-
ficient in his hands
- BENJAMIN TOMPKINS is allowed Sixty three pounds current money for rebuil-
ding & repairing the Warehouses at CONWAYs INSPECTION, which is ordered to be certified to the Treasurer of this Colony
- A Release from JOHN CARTER to JOHN TENNANT proved by the Oaths of MORDE-
CAI BUCKNER & JOHN BUCKNER Gent., and ordered to be certified

p.   Caroline County Court 9th of July 1772
83   - JOHN BAYLOR & JOHN (-NN) Plts. against WILLIAM SOUTHWORTH JUNR.
         Deft.   In Debt   On motion of the Plantifs by their Attorney, Judgment is
granted them against the said Defendant for their costs in this behalf expended
- GEORGE GAINES Plt. against WILLIAM REYNOLDS Defendant   In Debt
Came as well the Plantif by his Attorney as the Defendant by Note from under his hand
agrees that Judgment should be entered against him according to Bond; Therefore it is
considered by the Court that the Plantif recover against the said Defendant Eighty four
pounds eighteen shillings current money, the Debt in the Declaration mentioned; together with his costs in this behalf expended; and the said Defendant in Mercy &c., & this
Judgment except the costs is to be discharged by the payment of thirty two pounds nine
shillings with legal Interest from the 21st day of Janry. one thousand seven hundred
and seventy two til paid
- A Deed indented & Memorandum from JAMES BOWIE & ROBERT GILCHRIST Gent.
to JOHN MURIAH proved as to JAMES BOWIE by the Oaths of JAMES MILLER, JOHN
TENNANT & THOMAS SHIP, acknowledged by ROBERT GILCHRIST and ordered to be
recorded
- The Will of JOHN PALMER was proved by the Oath of MARY OLIVER and ordered
to be recorded. On motion of JOHN OLIVER (who having taken the Oath prescribed by
Law), Certificate for obtaining a Probate thereof is granted; Bond acknowledged &
ordered to be recorded
- Ordered ANTHONY NEWGENT, MELCHESEDECK BRAIME, BENJAMIN FAULKNER &
JOHN ELLISS, or any three of them, being first sworn, do appraise the Estate of JOHN
PALMER deceased & return an Inventory thereof to Court
- A Deed Poll from GEORGE PALMER to THOMAS OLIVER proved by the Oath of
JOHN OLIVER & the reacknowledgment by EDMUND PENDLETON Gent. & MICAJAH JONES &
ordered to be recorded

- Present GAWIN CORBIN & ROGER QUARLES Gent.
- The Will of GEORGE HOLLAWAY deceased proved by the Witnesses & ordered to be recorded. On motion of BETTY HOLLAWAY (who having taken the Oath prescribed by Law) Certificate for obtaining a Probate thereof is granted her, Bond acknowledged & ordered to be recorded
- Ordered that WILLIAM BUCKNER, GEORGE TODD, ANTHONY THORNTON & FRANCIS BUCKNER or any three of them (being first sworn) appraise the Estate of GEORGE HOLLAWAY deceased & return an Inventory thereof to Court.
- BETTY HOLLAWAY is appointed Guardian to her Son, CHARLES HOLLAWAY, Bond acknowledged & ordered to be recorded

p.   Caroline County Court 9th of July 1772
84   - It is ordered that JAMES TAYLOR Gent., Treasurer of this County, pay BENJA-
MIN TOMPKINS forty shillings for repairing GUINEAS BRIDGES
- A Deed Indented, memorandum & Receipt from THOMAS ALCOCK & FANNEY his Wife (she being first privately examined) to THOMAS TERRILL acknowledged & ordered to be recorded
- EDWARD POWERS Plt. against THOMAS SHIP Deft.   Trespass
Dismissed, agreed
- Ordered THOMAS LOWRY & JAMES UPSHAW Gent., in conjunction with EDMUND PENDLETON, JAMES TAYLOR & WALKER TALIAFERRO Gent., or any three of them. settle with ROBERT & BENJAMIN JOHNSTONs Exors. of WILLIAM JOHNSTON deceased, their Account of Executorship of the Decedants Estate & make report to Court
- JOHN GLASSELL Plantif against JAMES DUVAL Defendant   In Debt
On motion of the Plantif by his Attorney, Judgment is granted him against the said Defendant for his costs by him in this behalf expended
- JOSEPH GATEWOOD against RICHARD WATERS   On Petition
Came the parties by their Attorneys, & for reasons appearing to the Court, the same is redocketed & by consent all matters in dispute relative to this suit is referred to the final determination JAMES UPSHAW Gent., whose award is to be returned & made the Judgment of this Court
- Ordered the Sherif summon SUSANNA HACKETT, Widow of JOHN HACKETT deceased, to appear at the next Court to declare whether she will admininster on her said Husbands Estate or not
- ANTHONY NEWGENT took the usual Oaths to his Majestys person & Government, repeated & subscribed the Test, & was sworn as a Justice of the Peace in Common Law, Chancery & Oyer & Terminer
- WILLIAM ABBOTT against ANN MITCHELL   On Petition
On motion of the Defendant by her Attorney, It is ordered that this cause be redocketed & in the name of JAMES ABBOTT, Petitioner
- A Deed Indented from THOMAS BURK to REUBIN GATEWOOD acknowledged, & a Memorandum from HENRY BURK proved by the witnesses which are admitted to Record

p.   Caroline County Court 9th of July 1772
85   - On motion of THOMAS LOMAX Gent., (who having taken the Oath prescribed
        by Law), Certificate for obtaining Letters of Administration is granted him,
Bond acknowledged & ordered to be recorded
- Ordered ROBERT GILCHRIST, EDWARD DIXON, JOHN TENNANT & JOHN BOUTWELL or any three of them being first sworn appraise the Estate of LUNSFORD LOMAX Gent., deceased, & report to Court

- Ordered JAMES TAYLOR Gent., ROBERT GARROTT, HENRY WARE & THOMAS ALCOCK, or any two of them, settle with the Executors of WILLIAM DISMUKES deceased their Accounts of Exor:ship of the Decedants Estate & report to Court

- On motion of WILLIAM BOWLER, Attorney for JOHN JOHNSTON, Judgment is granted the Plant. JOHN JOHNSTON, against ZACHARIAH BURNLEY for two pounds ten shillings, also his costs in this behalf expended, for not returning an Execution which the said Plantif obtained against HARRY WINSLOW, the Defendant having had legal notice of the motion

- THOMAS RALLINS by JEREMIAH RALLINS, his next Friend against JOHN ROY Defendant In Debt Came as well the Plantiff by his Attorney as the Defendant in his proper person, and the said Defendant agrees that Judgment should be entered against him for Eight pounds with Interest from the Ninth day of July one thousand seven hundred and seventy two til paid; It is therefore considered by the Court that the Plantif recover against the said Defendant the said sum of Eight pounds with Interest from the Ninth day of July one thousand seven hundred and seventy two til paid by the Defendant in manner & form aforesaid confessed, also his costs in this behalf expended. By consent of the Plantif, execution on this Judgment is ordered to be stayed til December next

- The Will of JOHN HALEY further proved by the Oath of MICHAEL YATES and ordered to be recorded

- JOHN PICKETT Plt. against MOLLY ASHBURN & JNO: DOWNER, Defendts. In Debt WILLIAM ARNOLD Special Bial for the Defendant, MOLLY, produced her in Court and delivered her up in discharge of his recognizance

- Ordered that MARY ASHBURN, Executrix of JOHN ASHBURN deced. give security for her Executorship of the Decedants Estate

- SAMUEL OVERTON & JAMES WINSTON, Exors. of CHARLES GOODALL deceased, against WILLIAM FLIPPO On Petition Came as well the Petitioners by their Attorney as the Defendant in his proper person and the said Defendant saith that he cannot deny the Alegations of the Petition; It is therefore considered by the Court that the Petitioners recover against the said

p. Caroline County Court 9th of July 1772
86 Defendant the sum of five pounds, the Debt in the Petition specified; also their costs by them in this behalf expended

- BENJAMIN ALSOP is appointed Overseer of the Road in the Room of BENJAMIN GLANTON

- JOHN SMITH SENR. is appointed Overseer of the Road in the Room of WILLIAM BUCKNER JUNR., Gent.

- HARRY CROUTCHER is appointed Overseer of the Road in the Room of PETER THORNTON

- JOHN JOHNSTON is appointed Overseer of the Road in the Room of JOSIAH SAMUEL

- WILLIAM ARNOLD is appointed Overseer of the Road in the Room of GEORGE YATES

- MESS PICKETT Plt. against DANIEL BARKSDALE Deft. This suit by consent of the parties by their Attorneys, referred to the final determination of JAMES TAYLOR & RICHARD JOHNSTON, who have returned their Award as followeth: Pursuant to an Order of Caroline Court, we have examined the Records of MESS PICKETT & DANIEL BARKSDALE & are of opinion that the said BARKSDALE be discharged from the Judgment obtained against him by the said PICKETT on payment of

the sum of Twelve pounds ten shillings & eleven pence, with the costs of suit. July the
9th 1772. which Award by order of the Court is definitive between the said parties
        - Ordered that the Court be adjourned til the Court in Course
        - The Minutes of the preceeding Orders were signed by
                                        WALKER TALIAFERRO, Gent.

p.   <u>At a Court held for Caroline County on Thursday the Thirteenth day of August</u>
87   <u>one thousand seven hundred & seventy two</u>
                        Present his Majestys Justices
        JAMES TAYLOR   JOHN BUCKNER
        WALKER TALIAFERRO   and   Gent.
        WILLIAM WOODFORD   JAMES UPSHAW

        - A Release from JNO: CARTER to JOHN TENNANT further proved by the Oath of
JOSEPH ROBINSON Gent., & ordered to be recorded
        - A Deed Indented from CORNELIUS NOELL & SARAH his Wife (she being first
privately examined) to JNO: BOUTWELL JR. acknowledged and ordered to be recorded
        - Present EDMUND PENDLETON & JNO: ARMISTEAD Gent.
        - Ordered the Treasurer of this County pay SAML: HARGROVE thirty five pounds
which was levied for the purpose of building Bridges at COOKS FORD
        - ROBERT GILCHRIST Gent., Plt. against JOSEPH REYNOLDS Deft. On Attachment
 Came the Plantif by his Attorney and ELIZABETH REYNOLDS, the Garnishee in this suit
being sworn & examined declared the Defendant was indebted to her Five shillings &
seven pence, but that the said Defendant after her death is intituled to one tenth part of
his Father, CORNELIUS REYNOLDS, Estate, which she has in her hands, and the said
Defendant being solemnly called failed to appear and replevy the same; Therefore it is
considered by the Court that the Plantif recover against the said Deft., Twenty three
pounds nine shillings & seven pence half penny & all costs in this behalf expended, &
it is ordered that the Sherif make sale of the Defendants Right to his Father's Estate in
the Garnishee's hands or as much thereof to satisfy the Plantif his Debt & cost
        - BURNLEY & BRACKENRIDGE Plts. against WILLIAM FULCHER Deft.   In Case

p.   <u>Caroline County Court 13th of August 1772</u>
88   JOHN HAMPTON, who was security for the Defendants appearance produced the
        Defendant in Court in discharge of his recognizance, the Plantif moved that he
might be ruled to give Special Bail wherein the Defendant made default; On motion of
the said Plantif, It is ordered that the said Defendant be and remain in Custody of the
Sherif until he be legally discharged and the said Defendant prays leave til the next
Court to consider of & answer the Plantifs Writ and Declaration which is granted him
        - An Inventory of the Estate of JNO: PALMER deced. returned & ordered to be
recorded
        - Present GEORGE GUY & ANTHONY NEWGENT
        - A Deed Indented from JNO: TAYLOR & JNO: PENN, Gent., Exors of MARY PUM-
PHRETT deceased to JOSEPH DEGARNETT JR. acknowledged & ordered to be recorded
        - Ordered the Church Wardens of Drysdale Parish bind our JOHN WHALING,
Orphan of JNO: WHALING deced. according to Law
        - BURNLEY & BRACKENRIDGE Plts. against WILLIAM FULCHER Deft. In Case
JNO: HAMPTON entered himself Special Bail for the Defendant according to Law
        - JOHN PICKETT SENR. deced. Account of Executorship of JNO: PICKETT the Elder
deceased returned & ordered to be recorded

- WILLIAM PEMBERTON Plt. against JOSEPH DEJARNETT & NATHL: NORMENT
Defts.   JOSEPH DEJARNETT JUNR. entered himself Special Bail for the Defendants
according to Law
- Present ANTHONY THORNTON & ROBT. GILCHRIST, Gt.
- The Will of RICHD: WEST deceased was prov'd by the witnesses & ordered to be
recorded; On motion of CHARLES WEST, the Executor therein named, who having taken
the Oath prescribed by Law, Certificate for obtaining a Probate thereof is granted him,
Bond acknowledged & ordered to be recorded

p.   Caroline County Court 13th of August 1772
89   - Ordered GEORGE GUY, JEREMIAH RAWLINS, JOHN BAYNHAM & WILLIAM
PEATROSS (being first sworn) do appraise the Estate of RICHARD WEST deced.
according to Law
- An Inventory of the Estate of JOHN HALEY deced. returned & ordered to be
recorded
- WILLIAM PARKER, THOMAS LOWRY & JOHN MINOR, Gent.,took the usual Oaths
to his Majestys person & Government, repeated & subscribed the Test, & was sworn as
Justices of the Peace in Common Law, Chancery & Oyer & Terminer
- EDMUND PENDLETON, ANTHONY THORNTON, JAMES TAYLOR, THOMAS LOWRY &
JAMES UPSHAW Gent., took the usual Oaths to his Majestys person & Government, re-
peated & subscribed the Test, the said PENDLETON, THORNTON & TAYLOR as Colonels and
the said LOWRY as Major & UPSHAW Captain in the Militia
- ANN HART Plt. against JEREMIAH PEARCE Deft.   In Case
Came the parties by their Attorneys and it is mutually agreed that all matters in dif-
ference between them relating to this suit be referred to the final determination of
JAMES TAYLOR & SAML: HAWES Gent., whose award is to be returned & entered the
Judgment of this Court
- Present JAMES MILLER, JNO: BUCKNER JOHN ARMISTEAD, WM: PARKER,
WILLIAM BUCKNER JR., JNO: MINOR, THOMAS LOWRY, & GAWIN CORBIN Gent.
- A Deed Indented & Memorandum from MARTHA NODEN to JOHN GEORGE JUNR.
proved by the Oath of WM. SOUTHWORTH & JAMES YARBROUGH and by the Affirmation
of PLEASANT TERRILL & ordered to be recorded
- A Deed Indented and Memorandum from JNO: GEORGE to JNO: GEORGE JUNR.
prov'd by the Oaths of JAMES YARBROUGH & WILLIAM SOUTHWORTH and by the Affir-
mation of PLEASANT TERRILL & ordered to be recorded
- RICHARD ROY, JOHN CATLETT, JOHN ROY & JOHN BOUTWELL are recommended
to his Excellency the Governor as proper persons to be appointed Inspectors at ROYS
WAREHOUSE the ensuing year

p.   Caroline County Court 13th of August 1772
90   - THOMAS ALCOCK, ROBERT WARE & CHARLES TODD are recommended to his
Excellency the Governor as proper persons to be appointed Inspectors of
CONWAYS WAREHOUSE the ensuing year
- A Deed Indented from JOHN WALKER and Wife & JOHN JOHNSON to WILLIAM
FITZHUGH Esqr., Commission of MRS. WALKER. acknowledgment return'd and ordered to
be recorded
- A Deed Indented Memorandum & Receipt from CHILES TERRILL to ROBERT COBB
further proved by the Oath of THOMPSON MILLS & ordered to be recorded
- A Deed Indented & Receipt from HENRY WARE & MARTHA his Wife, she being
first privately examined, to RICHARD TAYLOR acknowledged & ordered to be recorded

- A Deed Indented & Receipt from ROBERT GARROTT & MARY his Wife, she being first privately examined, to RICHD: TAYLOR acknowledged & ordered to be recorded
- An Inventory and Appraisement of the Estate of JOSEPH REYNOLDS deced., in ORANGE County returned & ordered to be recorded
- ROBERT TALIAFERRO, WALKER TALIAFERRO & JAMES MILLER Gent., are recommended to his Excellency the Governor as proper persons to appoint one of them Sherif of this County
- JOHN COMER made choice of ROBERT TOMPKINS to be his Guardian, Bond acknowledged & ordered to be recorded
- On motion of THOMAS GARNETT, Administration on the Estate of LARKIN GARNETT deced., is granted him (DELPHIE GARNETT his Widow having relinquished her right of administration), oath administered, Bond acknowledged & ordered to be recorded
- Ordered ROBERT CHAPMAN, MAURICE KNIGHT, JAMES REDD & ROBERT HOUSTON or any three of them being first sworn do appraise the Estate of LARKIN GARNETT deced. according to Law
- A Power of Attorney from WILLIAM GOODALL to ROBERT MICKLEBERRY further proved by the Oath of JAMES DICKENSON & ordered to be recorded
- An Account of ANTHONY THORNTON Gent. Guardianship of HENRY TURNERs Estate return'd and ordered to be recorded

p.   Caroline County Court 13th of August 1772
91   - FRANCIS BABER return'd his Wards Account of RUSSELL & GEORGE GODBEY
        approved of by the Court & ordered to be recorded
- An Inventory of the Estate of JOHN MILLER JUNR. deced., return'd and ordered to be recorded
- JOHN MINOR Gent., return'd his Wards Account of AGATHY SWINNEY, LUCY CHEADLE, JACOB CHEADLE, THOMAS CHEADLE, JUDITH CHEADLE, GEORGE CHEADLE, ELIZA: CHEADLE, SALLY CHILES & URSLEY CHEADLE; approved of by the Court & ordered to be recorded
- The Will of WILLIAM TOMPKINS was prov'd by the Oath of JOHN SUMMERS & ordered to be certified; On motion of JNO: MINOR, BENJA: TOMPKINS & FRANCIS TOMPKINS (who having taken the Oath prescribed by Law) Certificate for obtaining a Probate thereof is granted them; Bond acknowledged & ordered to be recorded
- Ordered CARR McGHEE, SAML: REDD, JOHN CLARKE & JAMES DICKINSON, or any three of them, being first sworn, do appraise the Estate of WILLIAM TOMPKINS deced., according to Law
- On motion of GEORGE CHEADLE, is ordered the Clerk add his Tythes to the list taken by JNO: MINOR Gent.
- A Power of Attorney from ELIJAH DANIEL to ROBT: GILCHRIST Gent., prov'd by the Oath of WILLIAM DICKSON & WALKER TALIAFERRO and ordered to be recorded
- Ordered the Clerk add PATRICK CAFFRY to the List taken by JOHN MINOR Gentleman
- A Morgage Indented from WILLIAM BROWN JR. to ROBERT CHANDLER prov'd by the Oath of JNO: WILY & ANDW: LECKIE & ordered to be (erased)
- An Account of BENJAMIN JOHNSTON Administration of the Estate of WILLIAM JOHNSTON deced. return'd & ordered to be recorded
- DAVID STERN is appointed Overseer of the Road in the room of GILES NEWTON

- JAMES WARE by virtue of a Warrant from under the hand of ANTHY. THORN-
TON Gent. & pursuant to his recognizance appeared. The Court on hearing the Testimony are of opinion he is Guilty of suffering teaching & preaching contrary to the
Canons of the Church of England & a breach of the Act of Assembly prohibiting unlawful assemblies as in the Warrt: charged against him; It is therefore ordered that he
give security himself in the sum of Ten pounds & Two securitys in the sum of Five
pounds each for his good behaviour a year & a day

p.   Caroline County Court 13th of August 1772
92   - JAMES PITMAN by virtue of a Warrant from under the hand of ANTHONY
        THORNTON Gent. & pursuant to his recognizance appeared & confessed that there
was an Assembly of People met at his House to the number of Ten & endeavoured to
teach & preach as in the Warrant charged against him, which the Court adjudged to be
a breach of the Act of Assembly for prohibiting unlawful assemblies; Therefore it is
ordered that he give security himself in the sum of Ten pounds and two Securities in
the sum of Ten pounds each for his good behaviour a year & a day
        - JAMES WARE, JAMES PITMAN, WILLIAM TALIAFERRO & CHRISTOPHER SINGLE-
TON personally appeared & acknowledged themselves indebted to our Sovereign Lord
the King in the sum of Twenty pounds each to be levied of their several & respective
lands & chattels rendered in case the sd. JAMES WARE & JAMES PITMAN shall depart out
of the Prison Bounds til they give security in the sum of Ten pounds each with two
securities each in the sum of Five pounds each for their good behaviour twelve months
& day
        - ESTHER WILLARD Agst. WILLIAM MURRAH, Exor. of EDWARD MURRAH deced.
Petition for Freedom Dues   The Petition is dismissed by Order of the Plantif
        - JAMES TERRELL & CARR McGHEE, Exors. of JOHN COMER deced., against
JOHN HARRIS & JOHN JOHNSON Defts.   In Debt.   This suit is dismissed, agreed
        - JOHN CUMMIN Plt. against JAMES PATTIE Defendt. In Case, Slander   )
        - The Same Plantif against The Same Defendt. Assault & Battery   )
        - JAMES PATTIE Plt. against JOHN CUMMIN Defendt. In Case   )
Came the parties by their Attorneys and by consent, it is ordered that ANDREW LECKIE
in conjunction EDWARD DIXON, JOHN SKINER & JOHN TENNANT, the persons formerly
appointed to arbitrate these suits settle all matters of them be made the Judgment of the
Court
        - JOHN PENN Gent. agst. MUSE TAYLOR   On Petition
Dismissed, agreed

p.   Caroline County Court 13th of August 1772
93   - ALEXANDER PARKER Plt. against WILLIAM REYNOLDS Deft.   In Case
        On motion of the Plantif by his Attorney, Judgment is granted him against the
said Defendant for his costs in this behalf expended
        - JOHN TAYLOR & JOHN PENN against ANN ISBELL, Exrx. of DANIEL ISBELL
On Petition   Came the parties by their Attorneys, and on hearing the Testimony &
Arguments of each party, it is considered by the Court that the Petitioners recover
against the said Defendant one pound fourteen shillings and three pence, also their
costs in this behalf expended
        - WILLIAM BOWLER Plt. against JOHN TAYLOR Deft.   In Case
Came the parties by their Attorneys & a Jury to wit RICHARD ROY foreman &c., being
impanelled & sworn withdrew

- Ordered that the Court be adjourned til tomorrow morning nine O'clock
- The Minutes of the preceeding Orders were signed by

ANTHONY THORNTON Gent.

p.   <u>At a Court continued and held for Caroline County the fourteenth day of</u>
94   <u>August one thousand seven hundred and seventy two</u>
Present his Majestys Justices

ROBERT GILCHRIST	JAMES MILLER	
ANTHONY THORNTON	and	Gentlemen
JAMES TAYLOR	WILLIAM BUCKNER	

- On the Petition of ROBERT ROYSTON for leave to turn a Road, Ordered that BEN-
JAMIN ROBINSON, ALEXANDER ROAN, GILES SAMUEL & PETER SAUNDERSON, or any
three of them, (being first sworn) view the Road & report to the Court the
conveniences & inconveniences that may attend the alteration of the same
- MESS PICKETT Plt. against DANIEL BARKSDALE Deft.
Ordered the Clerk deliver the award in this suit to the Reference
- WEARS & WATSON against WILLIAM SUTTON   On Petition
By consent, ordered that THOMAS TREVILLIAN in conjunction with BENJAMIN
HUBBARD & PAUL THILMAN, the persons formerly appointed to arbitrate this suit, settle
all matters in difference between them and it is agreed that the award of any two shall
be made the Judgment of this Court
- Present WILLIAM WOODFORD, Gent.
- WILLIAM BOWLER Plt. against JOHN TAYLOR Defendt.   In Case
Yesterdays Jury in this suit being called & failing to appear, by consent of the parties,
a Juror is withdrawn & a new trial is granted them
- Ordered JOHN TAYLOR pay THOMAS POLLARD two hundred and forty pounds of
tobacco for attending this Court two days and coming & returning sixty five miles as
one shilling for ferriages as an evidence for him at the suit of WILLIAM BOWLER
- Ordered JOHN PENDLETON JUNR. pay ALEXANDER PARKER two hundred and
Eighty one pounds of tobacco for attending this Court three days & coming & returning
thirty six miles as an Evidence for him against JOHN WILY JUNR.
- Present EDMUND PENDLETON Gent.
- The Inspectors at ROYS WAREHOUSE returned an Account of the condition of
the Warehouses. It is ordered JAMES TAYLOR, ROBERT GILCHRIST & WILLIAM WOOD-
FORD Gent., or any two of them veiw & report what repairs are necessary to be made to
the said Warehouses
- Absent EDMD. PENDLETON, Gent.

p.   <u>Caroline County Court 14th of August 1772</u>
95   - JOHN TAYLOR & JOHN PENN, Exors. of MARY POMFRET deced., Compts.
       against WILLIAM PEMBERTON Defendant   In Chancery
Came the parties by their Council & on hearing the Bill, answers & Depositions &
sundry exhibits in this cause & arguments of Council on both sides, The Court are of
opinion that the Deed in the Bill mentioned was fraudulently obtained; Therefore it is
decreed & ordered that the said Deed be of none effect & that the Complainants recover
of the said Defendant their costs by them in this behalf expended from which Decree &
Opinion the Defendant prays leave to appeal to the (blank) day of the next General Court
which is granted him on giving security in the Clerks Office by the next Court
- Present EDMUND PENDLETON Gent.

- Ordered that the Court be adjourned til tomorrow morning nine O'clock
- The Minutes of the preceeding Orders were signed by
                              EDMUND PENDLETON, Gent.

At a Court continued & held for Caroline County the Fifteenth day of August
          one thousand seven hundred & seventy two
                    Present his Majestys Justices
          EDMUND PENDLETON   JAMES MILLER
          ROBERT GILCHRIST   and   Gent.
          JAMES TAYLOR   JOHN MINOR

- JAMES WIGNAL Plt. against WILLIAM JOHNSTON Deft.   In Debt
Came the Plantif and saith he cannot deny the Writing Obligatory in the Declaration
mentioned; Therefore it is considered by the Court that the Plantif recover against the
said Defendant the sum of one hundred and six pounds twelve shillings & ten pence, the
Debt in the Declaration mentioned, together with his costs in this behalf expended, And
the said Defendant in Mercy &c., But this Judgment except the costs is to be discharged
by the payment of Twenty seven pounds ten shillings & seven pence with legal Interest
from the thirteenth day of August one thousand seven hundred & seventy one til paid

p.   Caroline County Court 15th of August 1772
96   - ROBERT CHAPMAN (Quitam) Plt. against RICHARD SNEED Deft.   In Debt
        By consent of parties, this suit is dismissed
        - RICHARD SNEED Plt. against ROBERT CHAPMAN Deft.   In Case
By consent of parties, this suit is dismissed
        - BENJAMIN HUBBARD Plt. against WILLIAM JOHNSTON Deft. On Writ of Scire-
facias.   Came the parties by their Attorneys and the Defendant relinquishing his plea
acknowleges the Allegations of the Plantifs Writ, Therefore it is considered by the Court
that the Plantiff recover against the said Defendant three pounds two shillings & two
pence, one hundred & twelve pounds of nett tobo: & 15/, the Debt in the said Writ specified; together with his costs in this behalf expended
        - RICHARD YOUNG Plt. against JAMES BYRN   Trespass Assault and Battery
This suit is dismissed, agreed
        - JOHN TAYLOR Gent., Plt. against JAMES MILLER Gent. Deft. In Case
Dismissed, agreed
        - JAMES MILLER Gent. Plt. against JOHN TAYLOR Gent. Deft. In Case
Dismissed, agreed
        - GEORGE SMITH Plt. against JOHN & WILLIAM DICKENSON Defts. Trespass
Dismissed, agreed

p.   Caroline County Court 15th of August 1772
97   - Messrs. DUNLOPs & CROSSE Plts. against DAVID & PEYTON STERNs, Executors
        of CHARLES STERN dece., who was Exr. of RO. HALL, Defts.   In Case
Came the parties by their Attorneys and mutually agreed to wave the issue join'd in
this suit & submit the matter in dispute to the Judgment of the Court; Therefore it is
considered by the Court that the Plantif recover against the said Defendant seventeen
pounds fifteen shillings and also their costs in this behalf expended and the said Defendant in Mercy &c.
        - Ordered that ROBERT GILCHRIST, Gent., Exor. of JOHN MILLER JR. deced. pay
THOMAS SHIP one hundred & seventy five pounds of tobacco for attending this Court
seven days as an evidence for him against WM. JOHNSTON

- Ordered WM. JOHNSTON pay BEN: ALSOP one hundred & seventy five pounds of tobacco for attending this Court seven days as an evidence for him in the suit of ROBERT GILCHRIST, Exor. of JNO: MILLER JR. deced.

- JOHN GRAY & COMPANY Plts. against JAMES HEAD LYNCH Deft. Writ of Scirefacias. The Defendant who was Special Bail for WM: BROWN SENR. produced him in Court in discharge of his recognizance, On the motion of the Plantifs by their Attorney, It is ordered that the said WM. BROWN SENR. be and remain in Custody of the Sherif til he be legally discharged, And it is considered by the Court that the Plantifs recover against the said Defendant their costs by them in this behalf expended

- ANDREW COCKRANE & COMPY. Assee. of WILLIAM SNEED, Plts. against JAMES HEAD LYNCH Deft. Writ of Scirefacias on Recognizance
The Defendant who was Special Bail for WILLIAM BROWN SENR. produced him in Court in discharge of his Recognizance, On motion of the Plantifs by their Attorney, It is ordered that the said WM. BROWN SR. be and remain in Custody of the Sheriff til he be legally discharged, And it is ordered by the Court that Plantiffs recover against the said Defendant their costs by them in this behalf expended

p.   Caroline County Court 15th of August 1772
98   - JAMES RICHIE & COMPY. Plts. against JAMES MARTIN Deft. On Attachment
WILLIAM DAVIS in whose hands the Attachment was served being duly warned failed to appear tho: solemnly called to declare what of the Defendants Estate he has in his hands or had at the time of serving the Attachment therein; It is ordered that unless he appear at the next Court and declare as aforesaid, Judgment to be entered against him for the Plantifs Debt & costs

- The Honble. RICHARD CORBIN Esqr., Plt. against JOHN ARMISTEAD Gent. Deft. On a Protested Bill   The Defendant by Note from under his hand agrees that Judgment should be entered against him according to Bill; Therefore it is considered by the Court that the Plantif recover against the said Defendant Seventy pounds Sterling with ten per cent Interest then on from the fifth day of November one thousand seven hundred and seventy to the fifteenth day of August one thousand seven hundred & seventy two & seven shillings and seven pence Sterling with five per cent Interest on the whole from the Fifteenth day of August 1772 til paid, the Debt in the said Bill mentioned; also his costs in this behalf expended; And the said Defendant in Mercy &c., This Sterling Debt may be discharged in current money at twenty five pr: cent difference in Exchange

- WILLIAM ROGERS &c. Complaints. against THOMAS & RICE SCOTT Defendts. This day came the Plantifs by their Council and the Defendant RICE SCOTT being solemnly called failed to appear and answer the Complainants Bill, On motion of the Complaints. an Attachment for Contempt is awarded them against the said Defendant returnable to the next Court and demurer join'd with other Defendant and by their

p.   Caroline County Court 15th of August 1772
99   mutual consent, Commissions are awarded them to take the Depositions of their witnesses, giving each other legal notice of the time and place appointed for executing the same

- HARRY BEVERLEY Complt. against JOHN LINDSEY Deft. In Chancery
Came the parties by their Council and by their mutual consent, Commission are awarded them to take the Depositions of witnesses giving each other legal notice of the time and place appointed for executing the same & to be heard at the next Court

- BENJAMIN HUBBARD against ROBERT WRIGHT   On Petition
The Defendant by Note agrees that Judgment should be entered against him for One
pound eleven shillings with interest which he assumed to pay for MARGARETT WHITE;
On motion of the Petitioner by his Attorney, Judgment is granted him against the said
Defendant for three pounds seven shillings currt. money, being the Debt & Interest by
the Defendant confessed; also his costs in this behalf expended
        - JANE BUCKNER Complt. against JOSEPH ROBINSON Defendt. In Chancery
 - Came the parties by their Council and by their mutual consent Commission are
awarded them to take the Depositions of their witnesses giving each other legal notice
of the time and place appointed for executing the same & to be heard at the next Court
        - GEORGE PEAY Complt. against JANE THILMAN Defendt.   In Chancery
Same Order as last
        - ELIZABETH MERRIOTT &c., Exr. & Exrs. of OBADIAH MERRIOTT deced. against
RICHARD FORTUNE Deft.   In Chancery   Dismissed for want of prosecution

p.   Caroline County Court 15th of August 1772
100   - JOHN LEVELL against THOMAS SNODGRASS   On Petition
        Came the parties by their Attorneys and on hearing the evidence & arguments
of each part, it is considered by the Court that the Petition be dismissed and that the
Defendt. recover against the Petitioner his costs by him about his defence in this
behalf expended
        - WILLIAM PEMBERTON against THOMAS SNODGRASS   On Petition
 Came the parties by their Attorneys and on hearing the evidence and arguments of
each party, It is considered by the Court that the Petition be dismissed and that the Defendant recover against the said Petitioner his costs by him about his defence in this
behalf expended
        - Ordered that THOS: SNODGRASS pay WILLIAM WHITEFIELD one thousand and
thirty pounds of tobacco for attending this Court ten days and for coming and
returning sixty five miles as an evidence for him at the Petition of JNO: LEVELL
        - Ordered THOMAS SNODGRASS pay ELLISS SNODGRASS three hundred & seventy
five pounds of tobacco for attending this Court 15 days as an evidence for him at the
Petition of JNO: LEAVELL
        - Ordered THOMAS SNODGRASS pay DANIEL SCANDLAND three hundred and
seventy five pounds of tobacco for attending this Court fifteen days as an evidence for
him at the Petition of JNO: LEVELL
        - Absent ROBERT GILCHRIST Gent.
        - ROBERT GILCHRIST, Exr. of JNO: MILLER JR., deced., Plt. against DOCTOR WM:
JOHNSTON Deft.   In Case   Came the parties by their Attorneys and thereupon
came also a Jury, to wit, RICHD. ROY foreman &c., who were impanneled & sworn well
and truly to try the matter on issue join'd, do say that the Plaint hath sustained damages
by reason of the said Defendant to thirteen pounds twelve shillings currt. money;
Therefore it is considered by the Court that the Plantif recover agt. the said Defendant
his damages

p.   Caroline County Court 15th of August 1772
101   aforesaid by the Jurors in form aforesaid assessed, together with his costs in this
        behalf expended and the said Defendant in Mercy &c.
        - DOCTOR WILLIAM JOHNSTON Plt. against ROBERT GILCHRIST Gent. Exor. of JNO:
MILLER JR., deced., Deft.   In Case   Came the parties by their Attorneys and
thereupon also a Jury, to wit, RICHD: ROY foreman &c., who were impanelled and sworn

well and truly to try the matter on issue join'd, do say that the Defendt. is Not Guilty of
the Breach of Promise in the Declaration mentioned; Therefore it is considered by the
Court that the Defendant recover against the Plantif his costs by him about his defence
in this suit expended and that the Plantif take nothing by his Bill but for his false
clamour be in Mercy &c.

    - JOHN HACKETT deced., having been dead more than three months and no per-
son having applied for Administration on his Estate; It is ordered that the Sherif take
the Estate of the decedant into his possession and make sale thereof according to Law

    - WILLIAM TYLER & THOMAS DICKENSON, Gent., Churchwardens of St. Marys
Parish, Plts. against JOHN SUTTON, Deft. In Case   Pursuant to an award made &
return'd by JNO:MINOR & GEORGE GUY, Gent., It is considered by the Court that the Plantif recover against the said Defendant seven pounds nine shillings and four pence half
penny, together with their costs in this behalf expended, And the said Defendant in
Mercy &c.

    - Messrs. DUNLOPs & CROSSE Plts. against WILLIAM BROWN SENR. Deft.
In Debt on a Mortgage   The Defendant personally appeared and agreed that Judgment should be entered against him for Debt & Interest in Mortgage mentioned, On
motion of the Plts. by their Attorney, It is considered by the Court that they recover
against the said Defendant One hundred and forty six pounds sixteen shillings and
three pence with legal Interest from the first day of July one thousand seven hundred
and

p.   **Caroline County Court 15th of August 1772**
102   Seventy one til paid, the Debt in the Mortgage mentioned, also their costs in
    this behalf expended and the said Deft. in Mercy &c., The Defendant agrees to
release all Error of Proceedings in this suit

    - Messrs. DUNLOPs & CROSSE Plts. against WILLIAM BROWN SENR. Deft.
In Debt   The Defendant personally appeared and agreed that Judgment should be
entered against him according to Bond; On motion of the Plantifs by their Attorney, It is
considered by the Court that the Plantifs recover against the said Defendant Thirty four
pounds fourteen shillings & three pence, the Debt in the said Bond specified; together
with their costs in this behalf expended, and the said Defendant in Mercy &c., But this
Judgment except the costs is to be discharged by the payment of Seventeen pounds
seven shillings and one penny half penny with legal Interest from the twenty second
day of June one thousand seven hundred & seventy two til paid, The Defendant agrees
to release all Errors in the Proceedings in this suit

    - ROBERT FERGUSON Complt. against JAMES LOVERN, Deft.   In Chancery
Came the Complainant by his Council and the Defendant being solemnly called failed
to appear and file an answer to the Complainants Bill; On motion of the said Complainant, an Attachment for Contempt is awarded him against the said Defendant returnable to the next Court

    - GUSSEY VAUGHAN &c. Complts. against JOHN LEDFORD Defendt.
In Chancery   The same Order as last

    - HARRY BEVERLEY Plt. against DANIEL BARKSDALE Deft.   In Case
Came the parties by their Attorneys and thereupon came also a Jury

p.   **Caroline County Court 15th of August 1772**
103   to wit, THOMAS LAUGHLIN Foreman &c., who were impanelled and sworn well
    and truly to try the matter on issue join'd, do say that the Plantif hath sustained
damages by reason of the said Defendant to fifteen pounds, but it appearing to the Court

that the Plantifs demand arised by Gaming contrary to Act of Assembly, It is considered by the Court that the Verdict of the Jury be reversed and that Defendant recover against the Plantif his costs by him about his defence in this behalf expended

- GILPIN MOODY Plt. against ANN HAYNES Deft. Case for Slander

On motion of the Defendant by her Attorney, Judgment is granted her against the said Plantif for her costs by her about her defence in this behalf expended

- FRANCIS FLEMING, a witness for GILPIN MOODY against ANN HAYNES, failing to appear, It is the oppinion of the Court that he should be fined but as it is unknown whether the subpeanea was executed, the same is continued for proof

- JAMES BELL is appointed Overseer of the Road in the room of ROBERT CHEWNING

- EDMD. PENDLETON, THOMAS LOWRY & JAMES UPSHAW Gentlemen or any two of them are appointed to examine the Clerks Office and it is ordered that they make report thereof to Court

- Ordered that the Court be adjourned til the Court in Course

- The Minutes of the preceeding Orders were signed by
                        EDMUND PENDLETON, Gent.

p.   - At a Court held for Caroline County the Tenth day of September one thousand
104   seven hundred and seventy two
                    Present His Majestys Justices
         JAMES TAYLOR   THOMAS LOWRY
         WALKER TALIAFERRO   GEORGE GUY   Gent.
         WILLIAM WOODFORD   ANTHONY NEW

- Ordered that the Treasurer of this County pay JOHN WILY Ten pounds, it being the amount levied for him to be paid by Order of Court

- A Deed Indented from HENRY WHITE to DANIEL WHITE proved by the Oath of the witnesses thereto & ordered to be recorded

- A Deed Indented from JOHN MARTIN to ANN BLACKBURN and WALKER PEMBERTON acknowledged & ordered to be recorded

- Ordered WILLIAM TYLER, WALKER TALIAFERRO & JOHN MINOR Gent., & SAMUEL REDD or any two of them settle with RICHARD GOODALL his Account of Administration of the goods and chattels of CHARLES GOODALL the Elder deced., which remained unadministered by CHARLES GOODALL JUNR., deced., and report thereof to Court

- A Bill of Sale from JAMES LOVERN to (   ) & CAMBELL proved by the Oath of JAMES UPSHAW JUNR. & ordered to be recorded

- JOHN DICKENSON personally appeared in pursuance of his recognizance, and acknowledged with WM: (W-) his security to be bound unto our Sovereign Lord the King his heirs & successors in the sum of Ten pounds rendered in case the said JOHN DICKEN-SON shall not keep a Child of PATTY RIDDLEs which she made Oath was begot by him clear from the charge of Drysdale Parish or any other

- An Account of FRANCIS COLEMANs deced. Guardianship of JAMES SALEs Orphans, returned & ordered to be recorded

- BERNARD MOORE JUNR. Gent. took the usual Oaths to his Majestys person & Government, repeated & subscribed the Test and was sworn an Attorney at Law

- OWEN CARTER Plantif against JOHN GOODRICH Defendt.

Pursuant to an award made & returned by PEYTON STERN & RICHARD JOHNSTON, It is ordered by the Court that the Plantif recover against the said Defendant Two pounds ten shillings currt. money; also his costs in this behalf expended, And the said Defendant in Mercy &c.

p.   Caroline County Court 10th of September 1772
105   - THOMAS BURK Plt. against FREDERICK FORTSON Defendt.   In Case
The Defendant by Note from under his hand agrees that Judgment should be entered against him for Five pounds currt. money; Therefore it is considered by the Court that the Plantif recover against the said Defendant the said sum of Five pounds by the Defendant in manner & form aforesaid confessed together with his costs in this behalf expended. By consent of the Plantif, leave is granted the Defendant to make out any just Discount within two weeks
       - Present GAWIN CORBIN Gent.
       - JONATHAN GLANTON is appointed Overseer of the Road in the room of THOMAS SHIP JUNR.
       - A Deed Indented from EDMUND PENDLETON & PETER LYONS to WILLIAM PAGE acknowledged by EDMUND PENDLETON Gent. & proved as to PETER LYONS Gent. by the Oath of SAMUEL REDD & GARLAND ANDERSON & ordered to be recorded
       - JOSEPH GATEWOOD   against RICHARD WATERS   On Petition
 Pursuant to an Order made & returned by JAMES UPSHAW Gent., It is considered by the Court that the Petitioner recover against the said Defendant Two pounds sixteen shillings & four pence currt. money, also his costs in this behalf expended
       - On motion of JOHN SNEED JUNR., (who having taken the Oath prescribed by Law) Certificate for obtaining Letters of Administration on the Estate of WILLIAM SNEED deced., is granted him, Bond with security acknowledged according to Law
       - Ordered WILLIAM HORD, RICHARD BLANTON, THOMAS CROUCHER & HENRY MARTIN, or any three of them (being first sworn) appraise the Estate of WILLIAM SNEED deceasded according to Law
       - A Deed Indented from HENRY BURK to THOMAS BURK proved by the Oath of REUBEN GATEWOOD & JOHN ALEXANDER STILL & ordered to be certified
       - A Bill of Sale from JOHN THILMAN to ROBERT MICKLEBERRY, GEORGE GUY & JEREMIAH RAWLINS proved by the oath of WILLIAM SUTTON and JOHN YOUNG & ordered to be recorded
       - On the Peition of WILLIAM McGHEE for leave to turn a Road, ordered JOHN MINOR Gent., JOHN CHILES, THOMAS TERRELL & ROBERT COBB or any three of them, being first sworn, view the Road petitioned to have turned & report to Court the conveniences & inconveniences that may attend the same

p.   Caroline County Court 10th of September 1772
106   - JAMES RITCHIE & COMPY. Plts. against JAMES MARTIN Defendant
On Attachment   WILLIAM DAVIS, the Garnishee in this suit, being sworn & examined, declared that at the time the Sherif executed the Attachment in his hand, there was two feather beds, one chest & some pewter in his possession brought there by one SAMUEL GORDON, who has since carried the same away, and that he does not know whose Estate it was; On considering of which, it is considered by the Court that he be discharged from the Common Order against him in this Attachment
       - An Indenture of Apprenticeship between THOMAS BUCKNER, Orphan of THOMAS BUCKNER deced., & GAWIN CORBIN Gent. approved of by the Court & ordered to be recorded
       - Present ANTHONY THORNTON Gent.

- JAMES RITCHIE & COMPY., Plantifs against JAMES MARTIN Defendt.
On Attachment   Came the parties by their Attorneys & the Defendant pleads Not Guilty with leave which the Plantifs joined & the trial thereof is referred til the next Court

- Present EDMUND PENDLETON, ROBERT GILCHRIST & SAML: HAWES Gent.
- Our Sovereign Lord the King Plt. against THOMAS COLLINS, Deftendt.
On an Indictmt.   Came the parties by their Attorneys, & thereupon came also a Jury, to wit, JOHN BROADDUS foreman &c., who were impanelled and sworn well & truly to try the matter on issue joined, do say that the Defendt. is Guilty as in the Indictment charged against him; Therefore it is considered by the Court that the Defendant be fined Five pounds for the Breach found against him & that the Plantif recover against the said Defendant his costs by him in this behalf expended, And the said Defendant in Mercy &c.

- Ordered THOMAS LOWRY, JAMES UPSHAW, EDMUND PENDLETON JUNR. & JOHN BROADDUS, or any three of them being first sworn, appraise the Estate of JAMES JAMESON deced., which has come to the possession of MARY JAMESON, who obtained Administration de bonis non

- MARY DANIELs Representation of her wards Estate returned & approved of & ordered to be recorded

p.   Caroline County Court 10th of September 1772
107   - JOHN WALLER being brought before the Court pursuant to a Warrant, ack-
       nowledged the charge against him of his preaching at HENRY GOODLOEs; It is ordered he be & remain in Custody of the Sherif til he gives security himself in the sum of Fifty pounds & two securities in the sum of Twenty five pounds each for his good behaviour a year & day

- HENRY GOODLOE, pursuant to his Recognizance, appeared in Court & acknow-ledged that he was a Meeting of people to the number of Ten as in the Warrant charged against him which the Court are of opinion was a Breach of the Act of Assembly pro-hibiting unlawful assemblys, Therefore it is ordered that he be and remain in the Custody of the Sherif til he gives Bond for himself in the sum of Ten pounds & two securities in the sum of Five pounds each for his good behaviour a year & day

- For reasons appearing to the Court, NORMENT DICKEN is excused from not rendering an account of his Wards Estate at this day

- It appearing to the Court that ROBERT MICKLEBERRY, Guardian of THOS: HACKETT, has no charge against the Estate & that there is no Estate except a piece of Land on which his Wards Mother & the other Children of his Father liveth, is excused from rendering any account

- JACOB FENINGHOLTZ, Assignee of THOMAS NORMENT, Plt. against
MILES CANTY & JOHN GEORGE, Defts.   In Debt   The Defendant, GEORGE, per-sonally appeared & agreed that Judgment should be entered against him for Eight pounds, the Debt in the Bond mentioned; & four pounds four shillings & three pence for damages; On motion of the Plantif by his Attorney, it is considered by the Court that the Plantif recover against the Defendant & JOHN GEORGE, the sum of Eight pounds, the Debt in the Bond mentioned, & Four pounds four shillings & three pence for damages by the Defendant in manner & form aforesaid confessed, together with his costs in this behalf expended; & the Sherif having returned that the Defendt. was not to be found, the same is discontinued against him. By Consent of Plantif, execution on this Judg-ment is ordered to be stayed til Christmas

- The Account of JOHN PICKETT SENR., deced. for services against the Estate of

JOHN PICKETT the Elder deceas'd approved of by the Court & ordered to be recorded; & to be added to the Debit of his Executorship Account of the Estate of JOHN PICKETT the Elder deced.

p.   Caroline County Court 10th of September 1772
109   - JACOB FENINGHOLTZ, Assignee of THOMAS NORMENT, Plt. against
           MILES CANTY & JOHN GEORGE, Defts.   In Debt
The Plantif by his Attorney agreed to discharge JOHN PENN Gent. from his recognizance as Special Bail for the Deft. GEORGE
           - WILLIAM AYRES Plt. against PETER LANTOR & THOMAS PITMAN Defts.
   In Debt   Came the parties by their Attorneys & mutually agreed to submit all matters in difference between them relative to this suit to the final determination of EDMUND PENDLETON & JAMES TAYLOR, Gent., whose award is to be made the Judgment of this Court
           - A Deed Indented Memorandum & Receipt from WILLIAM BROWN SENR. to RICHARD GOODALL proved by the Oath of the witnesses thereto & ordered to be recorded
           - THOMAS ALCOCK pursuant to a Commission from his Excellency the Governor, repeated & subscribed the Test & was sworn as an Inspector of CONWAYS WAREHOUSE
           - SPENCER BOYD Plantif against JOSEPH LANGFORD Defendt.   On Replevin
   Bond.   The Defendant who had legal notice of this motion being solemnly called, failed to appear. On motion of the Plantif by his Attorney, Judgment is granted him against the said Defendant for Twenty six pounds four shillings, the Penalty of the said Bond, to be discharged by the payment of Thirteen pounds two shillings with legal Interest from the second day of June one thousand seven hundred & seventy two til paid & the costs of this motion
           - JAMES MILLER Plt. against MUNDLEY VAUGHN Deft. On Attachment
   HENRY STEWART, the Garnishee in this suit, being sworn & examined confessed he had One shilling & six pence of the Defendants Estate in his hands at the time of serving this Attachment therein
           - On motion of SARAH GAUNT (who having taken the Oaths prescribed by Law), Certificate for obtaining Letters of Administration on her Husband, JOSEPH GAUNT deced. Estate, is granted her, Bond acknowledged with security according to Law

p.   Caroline County Court 10th of September 1772
109   - Ordered THOMAS LOWRY Gent., LeROY HIPKINS, BENJAMIN SNEED & JOHN
           SNEED or any three of them being first sworn appraise the Estate of JOSEPH
GAUNT deced. according to Law
   (The remainder of page 109 is blank.)

p.   At a Court continued and held for Caroline County the eleventh day of
110   September one thousand seven hundred & seventy two
                          Present His Majestys Justices
           EDMUND PENDLETON   ROBERT GILCHRIST
           WALKER TALIAFERRO   JOHN ARMISTEAD &   Gentlemen
           JAMES MILLER   WILLIAM BUCKNER JR.

           - PAUL THILMAN Executorship of the Estate of JOHN WOOLFOLK deced. returned & ordered to be recorded
           - Messrs. ROBERT and ROBERT BOGLEs & SCOTT, Plts. against BENJAMIN JOHN-
   STON Deft. In Case   Came the parties by their Attorneys and mutually agreed

to submit all matters in difference between them relative to this suit to the final determination of OLIVER TOWLES Gent., is to be returned and entered the Judgment of this
Court

- RICHARD HIPKINS Plt. against GEORGE MAJOR & JOSEPH REYNOLDS, Defts.
In Debt The former Writ in this suit not being executed, On the motion of the Plantif
by his Attorney, a new Writ is awarded him returnable to the next Court

- JOHN GLASSELL Plt. against JOHN BROWN Deft. In Debt
JAMES CONDUIT entered himself Special Bail for the Defendant according to Law, and
came the parties by their Attorneys and the Defendant prays oyer of the Writing Obligatory in the Declaration mentioned which is granted him

- HOLT RICHESON, Admor. of CHARLES SEATON deced., Assee. of ARCHD: GOVAN,
who was Assee. of JAMES REYNOLDS, Plantif, against JOHN SUTTON Defendant
In Debt Came the parties by their Attorneys, and the Defendant saving and reserving to himself all advantage of exception as well to the jurisdiction of the Court as to
the Plantifs Writ & Declaration and prays time til the next Court to consider of & answer
thereto, which is granted him

p.   Caroline County Court 11th day of September 1772
111   - WILLIAM HARRISON Plt. against JAMES DISMUKES Deft.   In Debt
        The Defendant being arrested and failed to appear, tho: solemnly called, On
motion of the Plantif by his Attorney, Its ordered that unless the Defendant appear at
the next Court and answer this suit, Judgment be entered against him and CHARLES
CULLIN, who was security for his appearance, for what shall appear due the Plantif and
costs

- The Same Plt. against JAMES LOVERN Deft.   In Debt
The Defendant being arrest and failing to appear tho solemnly called, On motion of the
Plantif by his Attorney, It is ordered that unless the Defendant appear at the next Court
and answer this suit; Judgment be entered against him & AMBROSE VAUGHAN JR. Security for his appearance, for what shall appear due the Plantif & costs

- JAMES BOWIE JR. Plt. against JOHN GRIFFIN Deft.   In Case
The Defendant being arrested and failing to appear tho: solemnly called. On motion of
the Plantif by his Attorney, It is ordered that unless the Defendant appear at next Court
and answer this suit, Judgment be entered against him and WM. TOOMBS, Security for
his appearance, for what shall appear due the Plantif and costs

- ROBERT JERDINE Plt. against RICHARD JOHNSTON Deft. In Debt
OLIVER TOWLES Gent., entered himself Special Bail for the Defendant according to Law;
& came the parties by their Attorneys and the Defendant prays oyer of the Writing
Obligatory in the Declaration mentioned which is granted him

- WILLIAM ARNOLD Plt. against JOHN & CATHERINE TEMPLINE Defts.
Dismissed, agreed

p.   Caroline County Court 11th of September 1772
112   - ALEXANDER ROSE, Gent., Plt. against RICHARD STEVENS, Deft.   On Petition
        The Defendant being duly summoned and failing to appear tho: solemnly called
On motion of the Petitioner by his Attorney, Judgment is granted him against the said
Defendant for three pounds five shillings, the Debt in the Petition specified, also his
costs in this behalf expended

- JOSEPH DALTON against WILLIAM REYNOLDS   On Petition
The former summons on this Petition not be executed, On motion of the Petitioner by
his Attorney, a new summons is awarded him returnable to the next Court

- JOHN SOUTHWORTH against HUMPHREY EDMUNDSON   On Petition
On motion of the Petitioner by his Attorney, Judgment is granted him against the said
Defendant for his costs in this behalf expended
    - WM: LONG, Assignee of RICHARD JOHNSTON, Plt., against JOHN MILEAR JR.
Deft.   In Debt   The former Writ in this suit not being executed, On motion of the
Plantif by his Attorney, a new Writ is awarded him returnable to the next Court
    - WILLIAM BROWN JR. Plt. against CHARLES CULLIN, CORNELIUS VAUGHAN and
JOHN JOHNSTON, Defts.   In Debt   Came the parties by their Attorneys and the
Defendts. pray oyer of the Writing Obligatory in the Declaration mentioned which is
granted them
    - JOSEPH PRIOR Plt. against WILLIAM BROWN JR. Deft.   On Petition
The Defendant being duly summoned and failing to appear tho: solemnly called, On
motion of the Petitioner by his Attorney, Judgment is granted him against the said
Defendant for three pounds with Interest from the first day of January one thousand
seven hundred & seventy two til paid, the Debt in the Petition specified; also his costs in
this behalf expended

p.   Caroline County Court 11th of September 1772
113   - SPENCER BOYD against AMBROSE RAINES   On Petition
    The Sherif having return'd that the Defendant was not an Inhabitant of this
County, this Petition abates by his return
    - JOHN PENN Gent., against STEPHEN FORTSON   On Petition
The Defendant being duly summoned & failing to appear tho: solemnly called, On
motion of the Plantif by his Attorney, Judgment is granted him against the said Defendant for three pounds with legal interest from the sixteenth day of March one thousand
seven hundred and seventy two til paid, the Debt in the Petition specified, also their
costs in this behalf expended
    - JOHN GRAY & COMPY. against JOHN MILEAR, Admr. of JNO: MILEAR deced.,
On Petition   The Defendant being duly summoned & failing to appear tho: solemnly
called. On motion of the Petitioners by their Attorney, Judgment is granted them
against the said Defendant for Two pounds nineteen shillings and ten pence half penny
the Debt in the Petition specified; also their costs in this behalf expended
    - JOHN SANDERS against GEORGE GIBSON   On Petition
The Defendant being duly summoned & failing to appear tho: solemnly called, On
motion of the Petitioner by his Attorney, Judgment is granted him against the said
Defendant for two pounds sixteen shillngs & six pence, the Debt in the Petition specified; also his costs in this behalf expended
    - WILLIAM TIGNOR Plt. against WILLIAM GOODALL Deft.   In Debt
The former process in this suit not being executed, On motion of the Plantif by his
Attorney, an Attachment against the Estate of the said Defendant is awarded him
returnable to the next Court

p.   Caroline County Court 11th of September 1772
114   - EDWARD DIXON Gent., against JOHN MILEAR, Admr. of JNO: MILEAR deced.,
    On Petition   The Defendant being duly summoned & failing to appear tho:
solemnly called, On motion of the Petitioner by his Attorney, Judgment is granted him
against the said Defendant for three pounds eighteen shillings and one penny, the Debt
in the Petition specified, also his costs in this behalf expended
    - Messrs. DUNLOPs & CROSSE Plts. against JOHN FIELDS, Deft.   In Case
The Defendant being arrested & failing to appear tho: solemnly called, On motion of

the Plantifs by their Attorney, It is ordered that unless the Defendant appear at the
next Court and answer this suit, Judgment be entered against him & JAMES CARTER,
security for his appearance, for what shall appear to be due the Plantif & costs
        - Messrs. DUNLOPs & CROSSe Plts. against WILLIAM BROWN JR. Deft. In Case
  The Defendant being arrested & failing to appear tho: solemnly called, On motion of
the Plantifs by their Attorneys, It is ordered that unless the Defendant appear at the
next Court and answer the suit, Judgment be entered against him & ROBERT CHANDLER,
Security for his appearance, for what shall appear to be due the Plantif & costs
        - JAMES DICKENSON Plt. against JOHN THILMAN Deft.   In Debt
  The Defendant being arrested & failing to appear tho: solemnly called, On motion of
the Plantif by his Attorney, It is ordered that unless the Defendant appear at the next
Court and answer this suit, Judgment be entered against him for what shall appear to be
due the Plantif & costs

p.   Caroline County Court 11th of September 1772
115   - JOHN ARMISTEAD & NATHANIEL BURWELL, Gent., Executors of JNO: BAYLOR
        Esqr., deceased, Plantifs against JOHN BROUGHILL Deft.   In Debt
  The Defendant being arresting and failing to appear tho: solemnly called, On motion of
the Plantifs by their Attorney, It is ordered that unless the Defendant appear at the
next Court and answer this suit, Judgment be entered against him and WILLIAM
BROUGHILL, security for his appearance, for what shall appear to be due the Plantifs &
costs
        - JAMES RICHIE & COMPY. Plts. against SAML: MAJOR SENR. Deft. In Case
  The Defendant being arrested and failing to appear tho: solemnly called, On motion of
the Plantif by his Attorney, It is ordered that unless the Defendant appear at the next
Court and answer this suit, Judgment be entered against him and JOHN MURRAH, security for his appearannce, for what shall appear to be due the Plantifs & costs
        - WILLIAM MITCHELL, Assee. of JAMES LYLE Plt. against JOHN HARRISS Deft.
  In Debt   The Defendant being arrested and failing to appear tho: solemnly called, On
motion of the Plantif by his Attorney, Judgment is granted him against the said Defendant and JEREMIAH RAWLINS, Security for his appearance, for what shall appear to be
due the Plantif & costs unless he appear at the next Court & answer this suit
        - JAMES JOHNSTON Plantif against ELLISS GRAVATT Defendt.   In Case
Came the parties by their Attorneys and the Defendant saving & reserving to himself
all advantage of exception as well to the Jurisdiction of the Court as to the Plantifs Writ
& Declaration and prays time til the next Court to answer thereto which is granted him
        - JAMES CONDUIT, Admor. of the Goods and Chattles of NATHL: CONDUIT deced,
Unadministered by THOMAS CONDUIT deced. Plantif against JOHN BILLUPS & JOHN
WEBSTER Defendts   In Debt

p.   Caroline County Court 11th of September 1772
116   The Defendants personally appeared and agreed that Judgment should be
        entered against them according to Bond; Therefore it is considered by the Court
that the Plantif recover against the said Defendants seven pounds currt. money, the
Debt in the Declaration mentioned; Also his costs in this behalf expended; This Judgment except the costs is to be discharged by the payment of three pounds eleven shillings currt. money with legal Interest from the twenty seventh day of March 1772 til
paid, By consent of the Plantif, execution on this Judgment is stayed til Christmas
        - JAMES CONDUIT, Admor. of the Goods & Chattles of NATHANIEL CONDUIT deced.,
Unadministerd by THOS: CONDUIT, deced., Plt. against OLIVER SEAGOR & JOHN

DISMUKES Defendants;   In Debt. On motion of the Plantif by his Attorney, Judgment is granted him against the said Defendants for his costs by him in this behalf expended
      - The Same against MESS PICKETT JR., JNO: WEBSTER & MESS PICKETT SENR.
Defts. In Debt   The Defendants personally appeared and agreed that Judgment should be entered against them according to Bond; Therefore it is considered by the Court that the Plaintif recover against the said Defendants the sum of five pounds ten shillings currt. money, the Debt in the Declaration mentioned; also his costs in this behalf expended; and the said Defendants in Mercy &c., This Judgment except the costs to be discharged by the payment of two pounds eleven shillings with legal interest from the twenty seventh day of March 1772 til paid
      - EDWD. DIXON Gent., Plt. against JOHN GRIFFIN, Defendt.   In Case
Came the parties by their Attorneys and the said Defendant saving & reserving to himself all advantage of exception as well to the Jurisdiction of the Court as to the Plantifs Writ & Declaration & prays time til the next Court to answer thereto which is granted him
      - RICHARD GOODALL Plt. against REUBEN SANDERS Deft.   In Case (for Sanders)
The parties having agreed this suit the same is dismissed

p.   Caroline County Court 11th of September 1772
117   - Messrs. MURDOCKs DONALDs & COMPY: Plts. against GARROTT HACKETT
      Defendant   In Debt   ROBERT MICKLEBERRY entered himself Special Bail for the Defendant according to Law, & came the parties by their Attorneys and the said Defendant prays oyer of the Writing Obligatory in the Declaration mentioned which is granted him
      - WILLIAM OLIVER Plantif against WILLIAM DESHAZO & COLEMAN ROSS
Defendts.   In Debt   The Defendants personally appeared & agreed that Judgment should be entered against them according to Bond; Therefore it is considered by the Court that the Plantif recover against the said Defendents thirteen pounds, the Debt in the Declaration mentioned; together with his costs by him in this behalf expended; and the said Defendants in Mercy &c., This Judgment except the costs is to be discharged by the payment of Six pounds ten shilllings with legal Interest from the first day of June 1771 til paid, deducting Eighteen shillings paid (blank)
      - WILLIAM OLIVER Plt. against JNO: OLIVER & MICHL: McDONALD Defts.
On Petition   The Defendant, McDONALD, being duly summoned and failing to appear tho: solemnly called, On motion of the Petitioner by his Attorney, Judgment is granted him against the said Defendt. MICHL: McDONALD, for two pounds with legal Interest from the first day of June 1772, til paid; the Debt in the Petition specified; also his costs in this behalf expended; And the Sherif having returned that the Defendant, OLIVER, was not to be found, the same is dismissed against him
      - JAMES BOWIE JUNR. against JOHN GRADY   On Petition
The Defendant being duly summoned & failing to appear tho: solemnly called, On motion of the Plantif by his Attorney, Judgment is granted him against the said Defendant for two pounds fifteen shillngs & six pence, the Debt in the Petition specified, also his costs in this behalf expended

p.   Caroline County Court 11th of September 1772
118   - Ordered that the Clerk add two tythes belonging to MOSES ROBINSON to the
      list taken by WILLIAM BUCKNER JR., Gent.
      - JOSEPH HOOMES, an Infant, by EDMD. PENDLETON Esqr. his Guardian Plantif, against FRANCIS FLEMING Defendt.   In Detinue   Came the parties by their Attor-

neys and the Defendant relinquishing his plea acknowledges the Plantifs action; Therefore it is considered by the Court that the Plantif recover against the said Defendant seven Negro slaves, that is to say, two men named Tom & Simon, two women named Moll & Truelove, & three boys named Ben, Phill & Sye, the several Negroes in the Declaration mentioned & if they may not be had, the sum of One hundred pounds for each the value thereof together with his costs in this behalf expended and the said Defendant in Mercy &c

- THOMAS WILD against RICHD. STEVENS, On Petition
Came the parties by their Attorneys and on hearing the evidence and arguments of each party, it is considered by the Court that the Plantif recover against the said Defendant One pound ten shillings & four pence, the Debt in the Petition specified, also his costs in this behalf expended

- JAMES BOWIE JUNR. Plt. against JAMES CHARLES Deft. On Attachment
WALTER ANDERSON, the Garnishee being sworn & examined declared he had in his hands four hundred & twenty two & one third pound of tobacco of the Defendants Estate but it appearing that he was engaged to pay for the Defendant to that amount, It is considered by the Court that he be released as Garnishee and that the same be dismissed

- JAMES MILLER Gent. against HUNDLEY BAUGHAN On Attachment
HENRY STEWART, a Garnishee in this suit, having declared that he

p.   Caroline County Court 11th of September 1772
119   had one shilling and seven pence in his hands and the Sherif having declared
        that he executed the same on a Chest and the Defendant being solemnly called
failed to appear & replevy the same; On motion of the Plantif by his Attorney, It is considered by the Court that the Plantif recover against the said Defendant Six pounds & three pence, the Debt in the Attachment mentioned; also his costs in this behalf expended. and the said Defendant in Mercy &c., Ordered the Garnishee pay the money in his hands to the Plantif & the Sherif make sale of the Attachment Effects and pay the money arising thereby to the Plantif in part of this his Judgment

- ROBERT JOHNSTONs Executorship Account of WM. JOHNSTON deced., Estate returned & ordered to be recorded

- RICHARD TUNSTALL Gent., Plt. against DANIEL BROWN Deft.
Ordered the Clerk fill up the Judgment for Twenty pounds nineteen shillings and two pence current money

- The Same Plt. against HUGH SANDERS Defendt.
Ordered the Clerk fill up the Judgment for Ten pounds thirteen shillings & five pence current money

- JACOB HUNDLEY Plt. against ROBERT WOOLFOLK (Mad) Defendt.
Assault & Battery By consent of parties this suit is dismissed

- WILLIAM FOX (Marriner) Plt. against RICHARD JERVICE & FREDERICK FORTSON
Defts. In Debt THOMAS BURK entered himself Special Bail for the Defendant, FORTSON, according to Law

p.   Caroline County Court 11th of September 1772
120   - DOCTOR WILLIAM JOHNSTON Plt. against MARGARET KENNER, Exrx. GEORGE
        KENNER deced., Deft. In Case Came the parties by their Attorneys and the
Defendant relinquishing her former plea acknowledges the Plantifs action so far as to Thirty pounds thirteen shillings and eleven pence currt. money; It is therefore considered by the Court that the Plantif recover against the said Defendant the sum of Thirty pounds thirteen shillings & eleven pence by the Defendant in manner & form

aforesaid confessed, also his costs in this behalf expended; On motion of the Defendant by her Attorney, an Injunction is granted her to stay the proceedings on this Judgment til the matter can be heard in Equity, and a Commission is awarded her to take the Deposition of JNO: BENSON, whos is alledged as Infirm, giving Plantif legal notice of the time and place appointed for taking the same

    - JOHN WILLIAMS Plt. against JOHN BELL Deflt.   Trespass

Came the parties by their Attorneys, thereupon came also a Jury, to wit,ROBERT JOHN-STON foreman &c., who were impanneled & sworn to try the matter on issue joined; do say that the Defendant is Not Guilty of the Trespass in the Declaration mentioned against him; Therefore it is considered by the Court that the Defendant recover against the Plantif his costs by him about his defence in this suit expended, and that the same be dismissed and the Defendant for his false clamour be in Mercy &c.

    - Ordered that JOHN BELL pay BEN: BALL two hundred & twenty five pounds of tobacco for attending this Court nine days as an evidence for him at the suit of WILLIAMS

    - Ordered that JOHN BELL pay PETER ZACHARY two hundred & twenty five pounds of tobacco for attending this Court nine days as an evidence for him at the suit of WILLIAMS

p.   Caroline County Court 11th of September 1772

121   - WILLIAM PEMBERTON hath produced a Bond with security for prosecuting an appeal with affect at the suit of JNO: TAYLOR & JOHN PENN, Gent., Executors of MARY PUMFRETT deced. which is approved of by the Court

    - JAMES RICHIE & COMPY. Plts. against GEORGE MAJOR Deft.   In Case

SAMUEL MAJOR SENR. entered himself Special Bail for the Defendant according to Law

    - The Will of MARY PICKETT deced. was proved by the Oath of JNO: PENN Gent. & ordered to be recorded

    - Pursuant to an Order of Caroline County Court, we have examined the Clerks Office and find the Books and Papers in good order and the entering &c , recording property kept up. Certified August thirteenth one thousand seven hundred & seventy two. EDMUND PENDLETON, JAMES UPSHAW, THOS: LOWRY

    - THOMAS SLAUGHTER Plt. against JAMES MILLER Gent. Deft.   In Case

Came the parties by their Attorneys and thereupon came also a Jury, to wit, ROBERT MICHLEBERRY foreman &c., who were impannelled & sworn well and truly to try the matter on issue join'd, do say that the Plt. hath sustained damages by reason of the said Defendant to Twelve pounds current money; Therefore it is considered by the Court that the Plantif recover against the said Defendant the Debt aforesaid by the Jurors in form & manner aforesaid assessed. also his costs in this behalf expended, & the said Defendant in Mercy &c., By consent of the Plantif, there is to be deducted Nine pounds of this Judgment

    - JAMES MILLER Gent., Plt. against THOMAS SLAUGHTER Deft.   In Case

Came the parties by their Attorneys and thereupon came also a Jury, to wit, ROBERT MICKLEBERRY, foreman &c., who were impanelled & sworn to well and truly try the matter on issue join'd, do say that the Defendant is Not Guilty of the Breach of Promise in the Declaration charged against him; Therefore it is considered by the Court that the Defendant recover of the Plantif his costs by him about his defence in this suit expended and that the Defendant take nothing by his Bill but for his false clamour be in Mercy &c.

p   <u>Caroline County Court 11th of September 1772</u>
122   - Ordered THOMAS SLAUGHTER pay CHARLES ROBINSON one hundred pounds of
           tobacco for attending this Court four days as an evidence for him at the suit of
JAMES MILLER Gent.

        - THOMAS ALCOCK Plt. against THOMAS PITMAN & JAS: CARTER Defts.   In Debt
The Defendants personally appeared & agreed that Judgment should be entered against
them according to Bond, Therefore it is considered by the Court that the Plantif recover
against the said Defendants twenty pounds five shillings, the Debt in the Declaration
mentioned, together with his costs in this behalf expended; This Judgment except the
costs is to be discharged by the payment of Ten pounds two shillings and six pence with
legal Interest from the thirteenth day of December one thousand seven hundred &
seventy one til paid. By consent of the Plantif, execution on this Judgment is stayed til
March Court next

        - JOHN ELLIOTT PAYNE Plt against MARY, JOHN & JAMES DISMUKES, Exrx. &
Exrs. of WILLIAM DISMUKES deceased, Defendants   On Petition
Came the parties by their Attorneys and on hearing the evidence and arguments of
each party, it is considered by the Court that the same be dismissed and that the Defendant recover of the Plantif their costs by them about their defence on this matter
expended

        - MATHEW DAVIS, Assee: of AQUILLA JOHNSTON Plt. against GARNETT HACKETT
Deft.   In Debt   RICHARD ROY entered himself Special Bail for the Defendant according to Law and the Defendant personally appeared and agreed that Judgment
should be entered against him according to Bond; Therefore it is considered by the
Court that the Plantif recover against the said Defendant Fourteen pounds twelve shillings & two pence, the Debt in the Declaration mentioned, also his costs in this behalf
expended, And the said Defendant in Mercy &c., This Judgment except the costs is to be
discharged by the payment of Seven pounds six shillings and one penny with Interest
from the fifteenth day of November one thousand seven hundred & Sixty nine til paid.
By consent of the Plantif Judgment is stayed til Christmas & Errors released

p.   <u>Caroline County Court 11th of September 1772</u>
123   - SAMUEL RICCARDS, ISRAEL MANDETT & COMPY. Assignees of BOHANNON &
           HAMILTON Complainants against JAMES LEDFORD, AMBROSE VAUGHN & MARY
his Wife; JOHN LEDFORD, JAMES LOVING & SALLY his Wife, HENRY MARTIN & ANN his
Wife, JOSEPH LEDFORD, AUGUSTINE VAUGHAN & CATY his Wife & POLLY LEDFORD Defendants   In Chancery   Came the parties by their Council and on hearing the Bill
answers & Depositions, the Court are of Opinion that the Bill of Sale from JAMES LED-
FORD to ELIZABETH GOALDER for the slaves in the Bill mentioned, Sabina, Sue, Sarah &
Harry and their increase was fraudulently made and that the said slaves with their increase is liable to satisfy the Plantifs, their demand; Therefore it is ordered that the
Complainants recover against the said Defendants One hundred & Sixty one pounds,
three shillings with Interest from the tenth day of February one thousand seven hundred & Fifty nine til paid; Fifteen shillings or one hundred and fifty pounds of tobacco,
three hundred & eighty two pounds of nett tobacco; also their costs in this behalf expended; Ordered EDMD. PENDLETON JR., THOMAS LOWRY & JAMES UPSHAW Gent., state
an account of the Plantifs demand and proportion it between the Defendants and report
to Court who are in possession of the slaves and increase before mentioned, And it is
also ordered that the Defendants deliver the said slaves if required to the Commissioners
or give sufficient security to see them forth coming when called for and the the Commissioners report thereof to Court

- ROBERT WARE repeated & subscribed the Test and was sworn an Inspector at CONWAYS WAREHOUSE
- RICHARD GOODALL Plt. against ROBERT MICKLEBERRY Deft.   In Case
By consent of parties, this cause is set to be heard at the next Court
- MOSES WEBSTER Plt. against JAMES REYNOLDS JR., Deft.   Case for Slander
Came the parties by their Attorneys and the Defendant agrees that Judgment

p.   Caroline County Court 11th of September 1772
124   should be entered against him for Two pounds ten shillings; Therefore it is
        considered by the Court that the Plantif recover against the said Defendant Two
pounds ten shillings by the Defendant in manner & form aforesaid confessed, also his
costs in this behalf expended; & the said Defendant in Mercy &c.
- EDWARD PHILLIPS Plt. against JACOB DANIEl Deft.   Trespass Assault &
Battery   On motion of the Plantif by his Attorney, Judgment is granted him
against the said Defendant for his costs by him in this behalf expended
- Ordered that the Court be adjourn'd til to morrow morning nine O'clock
- The Minutes of the preceedings Orders were signed by
                                    EDMUND PENDLETON, Gent.

(The remainder of this page is blank.)

p.   At a Court held for Caroline County on Saturday the Twelfth day of September
125   one thousand seven hundred & seventy two
                        Present His Majestys Justices
            EDMUND PENDLETON   JAMES MILLER &
            ROBERT GILCHRIST   WILLIAM BUCKNER JR.   Gentlemen

- THOMAS SCOTT Complainant against WILLIAM HARRISS & ROBERT SCOTT, Exrs.
of WILLIAM BRUMSKILL deced., Defendts.   In Chancery
The Defendant, ROBERT SCOTT, being duly served with the Process in this suit and
failing to appear tho: solemnly called, It is Decreed & ordered that he settle with WM.
TYLER. JNO:MINOR Gent. THOMAS DICKENSON, ROBT. MICKLEBERRY & JNO: THILMAN or
any three of them his Decedants Account of Executorship of the Estate of his Father;
JNO: BRUMSKILL deced., and that they report to Court what part of the Estate of the
deced. JNO: BRUMSKILL is due the Complainant, with this Proviso, that if the said Defendant shall file his answer at the next Court this Decree & Order to be void
- ROBERT HART Complainant against WILLIAM DUDLEY Defendant
In Chancery   The Defendant being duly served with the Process in this suit and
failing to appear tho: solemnly called, It is the opinion of the Court that the Complainants Bill be taken pro confesso; Therefore it is decreed & ordered that GEORGE GUY,
JEREMIAH RAWLINS, JNO: BAYNHAM & MELCHESEDECK BRAIME or any three of them
state an Account of what is due the Complainant on the Mortgage in the Bill mentioned
& report thereof to Court with the Proviso that if the said Defendant shall file his
answer at the next Court, this Decree & Order to be void
- JOHN TAYLOR & JOHN PENN Gent. Complts. against LODOWICK GEORGE
Defendt., In Chancery   The Defendant being duly served with the Process in this
suit and failing to appear tho: solemnly called; It is the opinion of the Court that the
Complainants Bill be taken pro confesso

p.   Caroline County Court 12th of September 1772
126   Therefore, it is decreed & ordered that the Complainants recover against the
        said Defendant Twenty six pounds eight shillings & four pence half penny, with

legal Interest thereon from the twenty fifty day of February one thousand seven hundred & sixty eight til paid, the Debt in the Mortgage mentioned, also their costs in this behalf expended; And it is also decreed & ordered that GEORGE GUY, JEREMIAH RAWLINS & JOSEPH RICHESON or any two of them make sale of the negroes in the Mortgage mentioned (to wit) Prudence, Temperance or so many thereof as will satisfy the Plantifs their Debt Interest & costs on the first week in December next on credit til the first of April, And that the said Defendant be foreclosed of all Equity of Redemption in the Estate so sold; Nevertheless if the said Defendant shall file his answer at the next Court, this Decree to be of none effect

- JOHN WILLIAMS Complt. against JNO: ELLIOTT PAYNE & WM: CHICK Defendts. In Chancery   Came the parties by their Attorneys and on motion of the Defendants leave is granted them to take the Depositions of their witnesses on giving the Complainants Attorney legal notice or any other person to be by him appointed of the time and place appointed for taking the same

- JOHN SCOOLER &c., Complts. against EDWD. DIXON Exr. FURLONG, Defendt. In Chancery   Came the parties by their Council & by their mutual consent, Commissioners are awarded them to take the Depositions of their witnesses giving each other legal notice of the time and place appointed for executing the same

- JOHN THILMAN Complt. against JOHN McDOUALL & ARCHIBALD GOVAN Defendts.   In Chancery

p.   Caroline County Court 12th of September 1772
127   Came the parties by their Attorneys and on hearing the Bill & the answer of ARCHD: GOVAN and arguments of Council on both sides, the Court are of opinion that on the Defendant, GOVAN, giving the Defendant security to perform what the Court shall hereafter decree, that this Injunction be disolved and that the Defendant be at liberty to proceed on his Judgment at Law against the Complainant

- RICHARD JOHNSTON, Exor. FRANCIS COLEMAN deced., Complt. against JOHN GRIFFIN Defendt.   In Chancery   Came the Complainant by his Council and the Defendant being solemnly called failed to appear and file an answer to the Complts. Bill; On motion of the said Complainant, an Attachment for Contempt is awarded him against the said Defendant returnable to the next Court

- REUBEN HUNDEN Complt. against JOHN NORMENT Defendant   In Chancery The same Order

- ALEXANDER BAINE Plt. against WILLIAM HIGGIN JR. Deft.   In Case The Plantif failing to appear & prosecute this suit; On motion of the Defendant by his Attorney, Judgment is granted him against the said Plantif for his costs by him in this behalf expended

- The Same Plantif against The Same Defendant   In Debt The Plantif failing to appear & prosecute this suit, On motion of the Defendant by his Attorney, Judgment is granted him against the said Plantif for his costs by him about his defence in this suit expended

- WILLIAM SEXTON against JOHN HUDDLESTON   On Petition The former summons on this Petition not being executed, On motion of the Petitioner by his Attorney, a new summons is awarded him returnable to the next Court

p.   Caroline County Court 12th of September 1772
128   - ANTHONY HADEN Plt. against JOHN FERGUSON Deft.   In Debt The Sherif having returned on the Attachment awarded the Plantif in this suit that he had levied the same on a Book of the Defendants Estate & the Defendant being

solemnly called failed to appear and replevy the same; Therefore it considered by the Court that the Plantif recover against the said Defendant the sum of six pounds five shillings with legal Interest from the tenth day of March one thousand seven hundred and sixty nine, the Debt in the Declaration mentioned, together with his costs in this behalf expended; And the Defendant in Mercy &c., By Consent of the Plantif, the Effects attached are ordered to be returned to the Defendant

- LeROY HIPKINS & SAML: HIPKINS, Executors of SAML: HIPKINS deceased Plts. against GEORGE MAJOR & SAML: MAJOR SENR. Defts.   In Debt
The Defendants being arrested & failing to appear tho: solemnly called, On motion of the Plantifs by their Attorney, It is considered by the Court that the Plantifs recover against the said Defendants Ten pounds four shillings and eight pence, the Debt in the Declaration specified also their costs in this behalf expended, And the said Defendants in Mercy &c., But this Judgment except the costs is to be discharged by the payment of Three pounds two shillings with legal Interest from the seventeenth day of August one thousand seven hundred and seventy til paid

- MUSCOE GARNETT & COMPY. Plts. against FRANCIS CHANDLER Deft.   In Case
The Defendant being arrested and failing to appear tho: solemnly called, On motion of the Plantfs by their Attorney, It is considered by the Court that the Plantifs ought to recover against the said Defendant and WM: GRYMES, Security for his appearance,their damages which they have sustained by reason of the Breach of Promise in the Declaration mentioned, but because it is unknown to the Court what damages the Plantifs may have sustained in that

p.   Caroline County Court 12th of September 1772
129   account, It is ordered that they may be enquired of by a Jury of By Standers at the next Court

- THOMAS SHIP JR., Plt. against WILLIAM TOOMBS Deft.   In Debt
The Defendant being arrested & failing to appear tho: again solemnly called, On motion of the Plantif by his Attorney, It is considered by the Court that the Plantif recover against the said Defendant & JOHN GRIFFIN, Security for his appearance, Eight pounds, the Debt in the Declaration mentioned, also his costs in this behalf expended; And the said Defendant in Mercy, &c., But this Judgment except the costs is to be discharged by the payment of Four pounds with legal Interest from the 6th day of January one thousand seven hundred and sixty eight til paid

- THOMAS SHIP JR., Plt. against WILLIAM TOOMBS Deft.   In Case
Came the Plantif by his Attorney and the Defendant being arrested tho: again solemnly called, It is considered by the Court that the Plantif ought to recover against the said Defendant & JNO: GRIFFIN, who was security for his appearance; his damages in the Declaation specified; but because it is unknown to the Court what damages the Plantif has sustained on that account, It is ordered that they be enquired of by a Jury of By Standers at the next Court

- ANTHONY & BETTY BOWCOCKs, Exor. & Exrx. of JAMES BOWCOCK deced., Plts. against JOHN LONG & JAMES JOHNSTON Defts.   In Debt
Came the Plantifs by their Attorney & the Defendants being arrested & failing to appear tho: again solemnly called, It is considered by the Court that the Plantifs recover against the said Defendants Five pounds twelve shillings, the Debt in the Declaration specified, together with their costs in this behalf expended; And the said Defendants in Mercy &c., But this Judgment except the costs is to be discharged by the payment of Two pounds sixteen shillings with legal Interest from the Twentieth day of June 1771 til paid

p.   Caroline County Court 12th of September 1772
130   - ANTHONY & BETTY BOWCOCKs, Exor. & Exrx. of JAMES BOWCOCK deced. Plts.
        against JOHN MILEAR JR. & JAMES JOHNSTON Defts.   In Debt
Came the Plantifs by their Attorney and the Defendants being arrested and failing to
appear tho: again solemnly called; It is considered by the Court that the Plantifs recover against the said Defendants Six pounds fourteen shillings, the Debt in the Declaration specified, together with their costs in this behalf expended, & the said Defendants
in Mercy &c., But this Judgment except the costs is to be discharg'd by the payment of
three pounds seven shillings with Interest from the seventeenth day of June 1771 til
paid
        - ELIZABETH SAMUEL Plt. against JOHN SULLENGER Deft. Trespass
This suit is dismissed by the Plantif
        - RICHD: JOHNSTON, Exor. of FRANCIS COLEMAN deced., Plt. against JOHN LONG
Defendant   In Case   Came the Plantif by his Attorney and the Defendant being
arrested failed to appear tho: solemnly called; It is considered by the Court that the
Plantif ought to recover against the said Defendant and RICHD: ROY, who was security
for his appearance, his damages which he has sustained by reason of the Breach of
Promise in the Declaration mentioned; but because it is unknown to the Court what
damages the Plantif has sustained on that account; It is ordered that they be enquired of
by a Jury of By Standers at the next Court
        - The Same Plt. against THOMAS PICKETT Deft.   In Case
Came the Plantif by his Attorney & the Defendant being arrested failed to appear tho:
solemnly called, It is considered by the Court that the Plantif ought to recover against
the said Defendant and THOMAS RIDDLE who was security for his appearance, his
damages which he has sustained by reason of the Breach of

p.   Caroline County Court 12th of September 1772
131   Promise in the Declaration mentioned, but because it is unknown to the Court
        what damages the Plantif has sustained on that account, It is ordered to be en-
quired of by a Jury of By Standers at next Court
        - The Same Plt. against JOHN GRIFFIN Deft.   In Case
Came the Plantif by his Attorney and the Defendant being arresed failed to appear tho:
solemnly called, It is considered by the Court that the Plantif ought to recover against
the said Defendant his damages which he has sustained by reason of the Breach of Promise in the Declaration mentioned; But because it is unknown to the Court what
damages the Plantif has sustained on that account, It is ordered that they be enquired of
by a Jury of By Standers at the next Court
        - The Same Plt. against JOHN SANDERS JR. Deft. In Case
Came the Plantif by his Attorney & the Defendant being arrested failed to appear tho:
solemnly called; It is considered by the Court that the Plantif ought to recover against
the said defendant his damages which he has sustained by reason of the Breach of Promise in the Declaration mentioned; But because it is unknown to the Court what
damages the Plantif has sustained on that account; It is ordered that they be enquired of
by a Jury of By Standers at the next Court
        - JAMES LANG Plt. against HENRY MARTIN, Deft.   In Case
Came the Plantif by his Attorney and the Defendant being arrested failed to appear
tho: solemnly called, It is considered by the Court that the Plantif ought to recover
against the said Defendant & ISRAEL SNEED, & JAMES GAUNT, who were security for his
appearance, his damages which he has sustained by reason of the Breach of Promise in
the Declaration

p.   <u>Caroline County Court 12th of September 1772</u>
132   mentioned but because it is unknown to the Court what damages the Plantif has
        sustained on that account, It is ordered that they be enquired of by a Jury of By
Standers at the next Court
        - JOHN GRAY & COMPY. Plts. against THOMAS BURK Deft.   In Case
   Came the Plantifs by their Attorney and the Defendant being arrested failed to appear
tho: solemnly called, It is considered by the Court that the Plantif ought to recover
against the said Defendant & HENRY BURK, who was security for his appearance, his
damages which he has sustained by reason of the Breach of Promise in the Declaration
mentioned; But because it is unknown to the Court what damages the Plantif has
sustained on that account, It is ordered that they be enquired of by a Jury of By
Standers at the next Court
        - RICHARD JOHNSTON, Exor. of FRANCIS COLEMAN, deced., Plt. against
ELLIOTT EMMERSON   On Petition   By consent of parties, this suit is referred to
the final determination of JAMES TAYLOR & WILLIAM BUCKNER JR., Gent., whose award
is to be return'd and made the Judgment of this Court
        - GEORGE DABNEY & BENJA: CLEVIAS SPILLER, Admors. of WILLIAM SPILLER
Gent. deceasded Plantifs against ARON JERVICE Defendant On a Writ of Scirefacias
   Came the Plantifs by their Attorney and the Defendant being duly warned failed to
appear tho: solemnly called; It is considered by the Court that the Plantifs recover
against the said Defendant thirteen pounds & fifteen shillings or one hundred & fifty
pounds of tobacco, the Debt in the said Writ specified; together with their costs in this
behalf expended & the said Defendant in Mercy &c.
        - ROBERT GARROTT Plt. against THOMAS SAMUEL Deft.   In Case
   On motion of the Plantif by his Attorney, Judgment is granted him against the said
Defendant for his costs by him in this behalf expended

p.   <u>Caroline County Court 12th of September 1772</u>
133   - Messrs. ROBERT & ROBERT BOGLEs & SCOTT Plts. against RICHARD JOHNSTON
        Exor. of FRANS: COLEMAN, deced., Deft.   In Case
   Came the parties by their Attorneys and the defendant saith he cannot deny the Plantifs action, Therefore it is considered by the Court that the Plantifs recover against the
said Defendant out of the Estate of the said Decedant, when sufficient thereof shall come
to his hand to be administered, the sum of Twenty eight pounds, also their costs in this
behalf expended
        - LEWIS TAYLOR, Assignee of HENRY LYNE JR., Plt. against HENRY MARTIN &
   JOHN MARTIN Defts.   In Debt   Came the Plantif by his Attorney and the
Defendant HENRY MARTIN being arrested failed to appear tho: again solemnly called; It
is considered by the Court that the Plantif recover against the said Defendant & ISRAEL
SNEED & JAMES GAUNT, who were security for his appearance, six pounds seventeen
shillings, the Debt in the Declaration specified, also his costs in this behalf expended,
And the said Defendant in Mercy &c., But this Judgment except the costs is to be discharged by the payment of three pounds eight shillings & six pence with legal Interest
thereon from the tenth day of April 1769, til paid
        - The Same Plt. against JOSEPH DEJARNETT & NATHL: NORMENT Defts. In Debt
   Came the Plantif by his Attorney and the Defendants being arrested failed to appear
tho: again solemnly called; It is considered by the Court that the Plantif recover against
the said Defendants & JOSEPH DEJARNETT JR., who was security for their appearance,
seventy four pounds, the Debt in the Declaration specified; also his costs in this behalf
expended & the said Defendants in Mercy &c., But this Judgment except the costs is to be

discharged by the payment of Twelve pounds with legal Interest from the first day of
January one thousand seven hundred and seventy one til paid

p.   Caroline County Court 12th of September 1772
134   - JOHN GEORGE Plt. against THOMAS BURK Deft.   Assault & Battery
          On motion of the Plantif by his Attorney, Judgment is granted him against the
said Defendant for his costs in this behalf expended
          - THOMAS HALEY Plt. against SAMUEL SALE Deft.   In Debt
Came the Plantif by his Attorney and the Defendant being arrested and failed to
appear tho: again solemnly called; It is considered by the Court that the Plantif recover
against the said Defendant & RICHARD JOHNSTON, who was security for his appearance,
Thirteen pounds, the Debt in the Declaration specified; also his costs in this behalf expended; & the said Defendant in Mercy &c., But this Judgment except the costs is to be
discharged by the payment of Six pounds Ten shillings with legal Interest from the
tenth day of June one thousand seven hundred & seventy one til paid.
          - GEORGE GUY Gent., Admor. of FARRELL & ANN HUGHS deced., Plt. against
RICHARD JERVICE & FREDERICK FORTSON Defts.   In Debt
Came the Plantif by his Attorney and the Defendants being arrested failing to appear
tho: solemnly called, It is considered by the Court that the Plantif recover against the
said Defendants and JNO: GATEWOOD & THOMAS BURK, who were securitys for their appearance, Forty three pounds thirteen shillings, the Debt in the Declaration specified;
also his costs in this behalf expended; But this Judgment except the costs is to be discharged by the payment of Twenty one pounds sixteen shillings & six pence with legal
Interest from the first day of June one thousand seven hundred & seventy one til paid
          - BAYLOR WALKER & WILLIAM FLEET, Gent., Exors. of JOHN SEMPLE Gent., deced.,
against CHRISTOPHER SINGLETON   On Petition   Came the parties by their Attorneys and on hearing the evidence and arguments of each, Judgment is granted the
Petitioners against

p.   Caroline County Court 12th of September 1772
135   the said Defendant for One pound ten shillings, the Debt in the Petition speci-
          fied; also their costs in this behalf expended
          - The Same against THOMAS REYNOLDS (School Master),   On Petition
Came the parties by their Attorneys and on hearing the evidence and arguments of
each, Judgment is granted the Petitioners against the said Defendant for Five pounds,
the Debt in the Petition specified; also their costs in this behalf expended
          - The Same against THOMAS PITMAN   On Petition
Came the parties by their Attorneys & on hearing the evidence and arguments of
each. Judgment is granted the Petitioners against the said Defendant for One pound ten
shillings, the Debt in the Petition specified, also their costs in this behalf expended
          - The Same against JAMES FARISH   On Petition
Came the parties by their Attorneys and on hearing the evidence & arguments of each
party, Judgment is granted the Petitioners against the said Defendant for one pounds
four shillings, the Debt in the Petition specified; also their costs in this behalf expended
          - The Same against JOSEPH DEJARNETT SENR.   On Petition
Came the parties by their Attorneys, and on hearing the evidence and arguments of
each part, Judgment is granted the Petitioners against the said Defendant for one pound
seventeen shillings & six pence the Debt in the Petition specified, also their costs in
this behalf expended

- The Same against CATHERINE LONG   On Petition
The Sherif having return'd that the Defendant was not an Inhabitant, the same is
dismissed

p.   Caroline County Court 12th of September 1772
136   - JOHN TURNER Plt. against JOHN HARVEY Deft.   In Case
       Came the parties by their Attorneys and by their consent, this Cause is referred
to the final determination of GEORGE GUY & JEREMIAH RAWLINS, Gent., And it is agreed
that if they disagree, that they should choose an Umpire who are to proceed without the
party failing to attend; provided he have legal notice of the time and place appointed
for determining the same
       - JOHN RICHARDS Plt. against JOHN RALLINS Deft.   In Debt
The Sherif having returned that the Defendant is not an Inhabitant, this suit is discontinued
       - GEORGE GUY Gent., Admor FARRELL & ANN HUGHS deced., Plt. against
FREDERICK FORTSON & THOMAS BURK, Defendants   In Debt   Came the
parties by their Attorneys and the Defendants agree that Judgment should be entered
against them according to Bond; Therefore it is considered by the Court that the Plantif
recover against the said Defendants seven pounds six shillings, the Debt in the Declaration specified; also his costs in this behalf expended, & the said Defendants in Mercy
&c., But this Judgment except the costs is to be discharged by the payment of Three
pounds thirteen shillings with interest from the first day of April one thousand seven
hundred & seventy one til paid
       - PHILLIP JOHNSTON, Admr. of THOMAS JOHNSTON deced., Plt. against
JAMES JOHNSTON, Deft.   In Detinue   Pursuant to an award made & return'd by
ROBERT GILCHRIST & JAMES MILLER Gent., It is considered by the Court that the Plantif
recover against the Defendant the Horse in the Declaration mentioned or Twelve
pounds, the value thereof, together with his costs in this behalf & the said Defendant in
Mercy &c.

p.   Caroline County Court 12th of September 1772
137   - LENORD HARRISON Plt. against CHRISTOPHER SINGLETON Deft.   In Case
       Came the parties by their Attorneys, and thereupon came also a Jury, to wit,
DANIEL BARKSDALE foreman &c., who were impannelled & sworn well & truly to try the
matter on issue join'd, do say that the Defendant is Not Guilty of the Breach of Promise
in the Declaration charged against him; Therefore it is considered by the Court that the
Defendant recover against the Plantif his costs by him in his defence in this suit expended and the Plantif take nothing by his Bill but for his false clamour be in Mercy
&c.
       - WILLIAM DUDLEY Plantif against ROBT. & BENJA: JOHNSTONs, Exors. of
WILLIAM JOHNSTON deced., Defts.   On Writ of Scirefacias
Came the parties by their Attorneys and the Defendants relinquishing their plea,
acknowledge the Obligation of the Plantifs Writ; Therefore it is considered by the Court
that the Plantif recover against the said Defendants Five pounds, Sixty pounds of nett
tobacco & seven shillings & six pence, the Debt in the said Writ specified; also his costs
in this behalf expended
       - FRANCIS FLEMING Plt. against WILLIAM HARRISON Deft.   In Case
By Consent of parties by their Attorneys, Commission is awarded to take the Deposition
of EDMUND PENDLETON Esqr.

- MURDOCK, DONALDs & COMPY., Plts. against THOMAS PITMAN Deft.   In Debt
Came the Plantifs by their Attorney, and the Defendant in his proper person saith that
he cannot deny the Plantifs action; Therefore it is considered by the Court that the
Plantifs recover against the said Defendant Forty seven pounds, the Debt in the
Declaration mentioned; also their costs in this behalf expended

p.   Caroline County Court 12th of September 1772
138   But this Judgment except the costs is to be discharged by the payment of Twen-
      ty three pounds nineteen shillings & three pence three farthings with legal
Interest from the Thirteenth day of June one thousand seven hundred & seven one til
paid; By consent of the Plantif, Execution on this Judgment is stayed til April Court
      - JAMES GOVAN Plt. against THOMAS PITMAN Deft.   In Case
Came the Plantif by his Attorney and the Defendant personally appeared & agreed that
Judgment should be entered against him according to Account; Therefore it is considered by the Court that the Plantif recover against the said Defendant eleven pounds
eighteen shillings & seven pence half penny by the Defendant in manner & form
aforesaid confessed, also his costs in this behalf expended; By consent of the Plantif,
Execution on this Judgment is stayed til April Court
      - ELIZABETH EMMERSON Plt. against THOMAS PICKETT Deft. Motion on
Replevy Bond   The Defendant who had legal notice of this motion being solemnly called failed to apear, On motion of the Plantif by her Attorney, Judgment is granted
her against the said Defendant for Twenty five pounds, the penalty of the said Bond; to
be discharged by the payment of Thirteen pounds & six pence with legal Interest from
the 12th day of March one thousand seven hundred & seventy two til paid & costs of this
motion
      - LAWRENCE TALIAFERRO, Gent. Plt. against JOSEPH JONES Gent., Deft.
In Debt   Dismissed, agreed, the Defendant paying costs
      - The Same Plt. against The Same Deft.   Same Order

p.   Caroline County Court 12th of September 1772
139   - JOSEPH RYLAND Plt. against HANNAH HERNDON, Exrx. JAS: HERNDON Deft.
Trespass   Abates by Plantifs death
      - RICHARD JERVICE Plt. against WILLIAM CHEWNING Deft. On Attachment
The former Process in this suit not being executed, On motion of the Plantif by his
Attorney, an Attachment is awarded him against the Estate of the said Defendant
returnable to the next Court
      - BENJAMIN HUBBARD Plt. against JOSEPH PRICE Deft.   On Attachment
Same Order
      - JOHN CRANE Plt. against JAMES GIMBOW Deft.   On Attachment
Same order
      - JAMES SHADDICK Plt. against JOHN BARBY Deft   In Case
Came the parties by their Attorneys, & the Defendant saving & reserving to himself all
manner of advantage of exception as well to the Jurisdiction of the Court as to the Plantifs Writ & Declartion and prays leave til the next Court to consider of & answer thereto
which is granted him
      - MARY STEVENS Plt. against WILLIAM GAUNT, Deft.   In Case
On motion of the Defendant by his Attorney, Judgment is granted him against the
Plantif for his costs about his defence in this suit expended
      - SAMUEL DANIEL & ELIZABETH CHEWNING, Witnesses for MARY STEVENS
against WILLIAM GAUNT being duly summoned failed to

p.   <u>Caroline County Court 12th of September 1772</u>
140   appear tho: solemnly called, It is ordered that they be fined according to Law
          unless they appear at the next Court and shew cause to the contrary
          - JOHN GRAY & COMPY. Plts. against CHARLES ROBINSON Deft.   On Attachment
The Sherif having returned on the Attachment that he levied the same on a parcell of
Household Goods & the said Defendant being solemnly called, failed to appear; On motion
of the Plantifs by their Attorney, Judgment is granted them against the said Defendant
for Twenty three pounds twelve shillings & six pence half penny, the Debt in the
Attachment specified; also their costs in this behalf expended; & the said Defendant in
Mercy &c., It is ordered that the Sherif make sale of the Effects by him attached and
pay the money arising thereby to the Plantifs towards satisfying this Judgment.
GEORGE MUSE and THOMAS SLAUGHTER, who were summoned as Garnishees in this suit
being solemnly called filed to appear and declare wht of the Estate of the Defendant
they had in their hands or had at the time of serving the Attachment therein; On
motion of the Plantifs by their Attorney, Attachment for Contempt is awarded them
returnable to the next Court
          - The Exor. of WILLIAM HUNTER deced., Plt. against LAWRENCE BATTAILE Deft.
In Case   The Order for reference in this suit is reversed and the Defendant pleads
non assumpsit which the Plantif joined & the trial thereof is refered til the next Court
          - LUNSFORD LOMAX Gent., Complt. against EDMUND PENDLETON & ALEX: ROSE
Gent., Exors. ROBERT INNIS deced. Defendts.   In Chancery
(This entry was not completed. There appears to be a missing page or pages, for the following page,
although numbered in sequence begins a new Court.)

p.   <u>At a Court held for Caroline County on Thursday the Eighth day of October</u>
141   <u>one thousand seven hundred & seventy two</u>
                        Present His Majestys Justices
          ROBERT GILCHRIST   WALKER TALIAFERRO
          ANTHONY THORNTON   JOHN ARMISTEAD   Gent.

          - Ordered WILLIAM TYLER, JNO: MINOR, ROGER QUARLES, ROBERT MICKLEBERRY
& SAMUEL WORTHAM Gent., or any two, view the Bridge built across PAMUNKEY RIVER
by SAMUEL HARGROVE and report to Court the value thereof and what they think the
maintainance of it seven years is worth
          - A Deed Indented from JNO: GEORGE (hhd.) and FRANCES his Wife (she being
first privately examined) to HUMPHREY HALEY acknowledged & ordered to be recorded
          - A Deed Indented from JNO: GEORGE (hhd.) & FRANCES his Wife (she being first
privately examined) to MATTHEW CRANK acknowledged & ordered to be recorded
          - ANTHONY THORNTON JUNR., Gent., pursuant to a Commission took the usual
oaths to his Majestys person & Government, repeated & subscribed the Test, and was
sworn a Captain in the Malitia
          - An Account of MARY FLETCHERs Administration of the Estate of ELIAS BLACK-
BURN deced., return'd & ordered to be recorded
          - A Deed Indented from HUMPHREY SINGLETON to WILLIAM BARLOW acknow-
ledged & ordered to be recorded
          - WILLIAM JOHNSTON Plt. against THOMAS ROY Deft.   In Case
 Came the parties by their Attorneys, and by their mutual consent all matters in difference between them relative to this suit be refered to the final determination of
JAMES TAYLOR, WILLIAM WOODFORD & JAMES DUNLOP Gent., or any two of them, whose
award is to be return'd & entered the Judgment of this Court

p.   <u>Caroline County Court 8th of October 1772</u>
141   (This page also is numbered 141 and contains only one entry as follows:)
        - By consent of the parties, this Proceedings in this suit is revised in the name
of THOMAS LOMAX Gent. Heir at Law (this entry not completed, the remainder of this page is
blank.)

p.   <u>Caroline County Court 8th of October 1772</u>
142   - DOCTR: WILLIAM JOHNSTON Plt. against RICHARD JOHNSTON, Exor. of
        FRANCIS COLEMAN, deced., Deft.   In Case   Came the parties by their
Attorneys and it is mutually agreed that all matters in difference between them rela-
tive to this suit be refered to the final determination of JAMES TAYLOR, WM. WOODFORD
& JAMES DUNLOP Gent., or any two, whose award is to be return'd & entered the Judg-
ment of this Court
        - RICHARD JOHNSTON, Exor. FRANCIS COLEMAN deced., Plt. against
DOCTOR WILLIAM JOHNSTON Deft.   In Case   The same order
        - LUCY LEWIS took the usual oath of an Executrix to the Will of CHARLES LEWIS
Gent., deced., Bond acknowledged & ordered to be recorded
        - Ordered ROBERT GILCHRIST, JAMES MILLER, JAMES DUNLOP, ANDREW LECKIE
& JNO: CATLETT, or any three of them, being first sworn, appraise the Estate of CHARLES
LEWIS Gent., deced. according to Law,
        - A Renunciation of LUCY LEWIS of her Husband, CHARLES LEWIS, Will proved
by the witnesses & ordered to be recorded
        - Ordered GEORGE GUY, ANTHONY NEW & JEREMIAH RAWLINS Gent. & MELCHESE-
DECK BRAME or any two, divide the Estate of JAMES SINGLETON deced., agreeable to his
Will & assign to the Widow her thirds thereof
        - A Deed Indented from FREDERICK FORTSON to STEPHEN FORTSON prov'd by the
oath of JNO: MOUNTAGUE & ordered to be recorded
        - NORMENT DICKEN return'd his account of JNO: WHITLOCKs Estate, sworn to,
approved of by the Court & ordered to be recorded
        - FRANCIS HALBERTs Account of MARTHA HALBERT return'd & ordered to be
recorded
        - A Commission & Certificate of Mrs. ANN MARSHALLs acknowledgment of a Deed
from herself & Husband to Revd. ARCHD: DICK return'd & ordered to be recorded
        - A Deed Indented from HENRY BURK to THOMAS BURK further prov'd by the
Oath of ANN BURK & ordered to be recorded

p.   <u>Caroline County Court 8th of October 1772</u>
143   - IGNATIOUS WEST made choice of SAMUEL BURRUS to be his Guardian, Bond
        acknowledged & ordered to be recorded
        - WILLIAM PEATROSS is appointed Guardian to JNO: WEST, Bond acknowledged &
ordered to be recorded
        - WILLIAM YOUNG is appointed Guardian to JOSEPH & ANNE WEST, Bond acknow-
ledged & ordered to be recorded
        - CHARLES WEST is appointed Guardian to WILLIAM & ALICE WEST, Bond acknow-
ledged & ordered to be recorded
        - Present GEORGE GUY Gent.
        - On motion of WILLIAM PRICE, Certificate for obtaining Letters of Administra-
tion on the Estate of AUGUSTIN ELLISS deced., is granted him, Oath administered, Bond
acknowledged & ordered to be recorded

- Ordered SAMUEL HAWES, AQUILLA JOHNSTON, GEORGE YATES & JOHN ESTIS or any three of them being first sworn appraise the Estate of AUGUSTIN ELLISS deced. according to Law

- A Deed Indented & Receipt from THOMAS RICHESON to JEREMIAH RAWLINS prov'd by the witnesses & ordered to be recorded

- The Will of LODOWICK MURRAH proved by the witnesses & ordered to be recorded; On motion of JNO: JETER (who having taken the Oath prescribed by Law) Certificate for obtaining a Probate thereof is granted him; Bond acknowledged & ordered to be recorded

- Ordered GILES SAMUEL, JAMES KAY, ROY GRIFFIN & JNO: EVANS, or any three of them, being first sworn, do appraise the Estate of LODOWICK MURRAH deced, according to Law

- JOHN WATTS is appointed Overseer of the Road in the room of RICHARD WOOL-FOLK

- BETTY CHEWNING is excused from the fines assessed against her for not attending at a suit, STEVENS against GAUNT

- On the Petition of HAMPTON RALL for Freedom; It is ordered that EDWD: STEVENS be summoned to appear at the next Court to answer thereto & leave is granted the Petitioner til next Court to get his security

- An Inventory of the Estate of WILLIAM SNEED deced. return'd & ordered to be recorded

p. Caroline County Court 8th of August 1772
144   - A Deed Indented & Receipt from EDWARD BRASFIELD & ELIZABETH his Wife (she being first privately examined) to BENJA: POE acknowledged, & ordered to be recorded

- A Deed of Lease & Release from NICHOLAS LONG to JAMES PATTIE prov'd by the Oaths of ROBT GILCHRIST Gent., WILLIAM DIXON, SAML. MAJOR JR. & ordered to be recorded

- An Indenture of Apprentice between BURRUS & YOUNG approved of by the Court & ordered to be recorded

- WILLIAM TYLER, ROGER QUARLES, BENJAMIN TOMPKINS & THOMAS TERRELL, or any three of them, are appointed to settle with the Exor. of JOHN CHEADLE deced., their Account of Executorship, also of THOS: CHEADLE

- JAMES DICKENSON Plt. against JOHN THILMAN Deft.   In JAMES HEAD LYNCH entered himself Special Bail for the Defendant according to Law

- A Deed Indented & Receipt from JOHN WALKER &c. to WM. FITZHUGH Esqr., further prov'd by the Oath of ARCHIBALD DICK

- A Deed Indented from WM. ROGERS &c. to ROBERT FARISH acknowledged (except by PLEASANT TERRELL) & the several parties Wifes being first privately examined & ordered to be Certified

- A Deed Indented from WM. ROGERS &c. to ROBERT FARISH acknowledged (except to PLEASANT TERRELL) and the several parties Wifes being privately examined, & ordered to be Certified

- A Deed Indented from THOMAS BURK to JNO: GATEWOOD acknowledged & ordered to be recorded

- RODHAM KENNER made choice of JAMES MILLER Gent. to be his Guardian, Bond acknowledged & ordered to be recorded

- Ordered JNO: HEWETT pay WILLIAM EUBANK twenty five pounds of tobacco for attending this Court one day as an evidence for him against JNO: PENN, Gent.

- Ordered THOMAS LOWRY, JAMES UPSHAW Gent. & JAMES GARNETT or any two of them settle with the Exors. of HENRY ANOMY deced. their Account of Exor:ship & report to Court

p.   Caroline County Court 8th of October 1772
145   - JOHN GRAY & COMPY. Plts. against CHARLES ROBINSON Deft. On Attachment
        GEORGE MUSE, the Garnishee in this suit being sworn & examined, declared that he has in his hands of the Defendants Estate one bed & furniture, one iron pott, three chairs, three plates, one dish, one bason, one hatchett, one tub & pail, some earthen cups & three bushells of Wheat. It is ordered that the Sherif make sale thereof and pay the money arising thereby to the Plantifs toward satisfying their Debt.

        Agreeable to an Order of Caroline County Court, we the Subscribers, being first qualified, have viewed the way now in use which runs through the Plantation of WILLIAM McGHEE & MOSES CARNALL considerably to their prejudice; we have also viewed the alteration proposed beginning where CARR McGHEEs Road comes into SWINNEYS ROAD, running a small distance along the said McGHEE's ROAD, thence along a Ridge across a sharp corner of THOMAS CHILES's Land to SWINNEYS & MARTINs Corner, then along the line between MARTIN & SWINNEY to McGHEEs corner, thence along McGHEEs line to SWINNEYs ROAD which we think very little further than the way now in use and may be as good and will be of very little prejudice to any person. Given under our hands this seventh day of October 1772; JOHN MINOR, JOHN CHILES & THOS: TERRELL, And it is considered by the Court that the way be established agreeable thereto

        - JAMES CONDUIT Plt. against ALEXANDER PARKER Deft.   In Debt
        Came the Plantif by his Attorney and the Defendant by Note from under his hand agrees that Judgment should be entered against him according to Bond; Therefore it is considered by the Court that the Plantif recover against the said Defendant Thirty six pounds, the Debt in the Declaration mentioned, together with his costs in this behalf expended; And the said Defendant in Mercy &c., But this Judgment except the costs is to be discharged by the payment of Eighteen pounds current money with legal Interest from the first day of May 1771 til paid

p.   Caroline County Court 8th of October 1772
146   - JOHN JOUITT, Assignee of ADAM DEAN, Plt. against AUGUSTIN MEEKS Deft.
        On Attachment   CHARLES WEST, the Garnishee in this suit being sworn & examined saith that he as Executor of RICHARD WEST deced. should have (when he could make sale of the Decedants Estate & receive the money arising thereby) sufficient in his hands to satisfy the Plantif his demand; And the Defendant being solemnly called failed to appear; On motion of the Plantif by his Attorney, Itis considered by the Court that the Plantif recover against the said Defendant Twenty two pounds currt. money with his costs in this behalf expended; & the said Defendant in Mercy &c., But this Judgment except the costs is to be discharged by the payment of Eleven pounds with legal Interest thereon from the first day of July 1769 til paid; one hundred & fifty five pounds of nett tobacco, fifteen shillings or one hundred and fifty pounds of tobacco & one shilling & three pence

        - The Inspectors at ROYS WAREHOUSE having reported to Court the state of their Warehouses, It is ordered that the Sherif summon JAMES MILLER Gent., the Proprietor thereof, to appear at the next Court to give Bond to make the necessary repairs

        - RICHARD ROY & JOHN CATLETT, Inspectors at ROYS WAREHOUSE, return'd an Account of Tobacco remaining in their hands amounting to one thousand two hundred & forty four which they were directed to make sale of & they having return'd that it sold for fifteen shillings p hundred

- MELCHESEDECK BRAME & RICHARD WYATT, Exors. of WALTER CHILES deced.
Plts. against ROBERT WOOLFOLK & FRANCIS BABER Defts.   In Debt
Came the Plantifs by their Attorney and the Defendant agrees that Judgment should be
entered against him according to Bond; Therefore it is considered by the Court that the
Plantifs recover against

p.   Caroline County Court 8th of October 1772
147   the said Defendants twenty two pounds four shillings, the Debt in the Declara-
        tion mentioned, together with their costs in this behalf expended; But this Judg-
ment except the costs is to be discharged by the payment of Eleven pouns two shillings
currt. money with legal Interest from the tenth day of June 1771 til paid
        - JOHN GRAY & CO., Plts. against CHARLES ROBINSON Deft.   On Attachment
THOMAS SLAUGHTER, Garnishee in this suit being sworn & examined declared he had
in his hands two hundred and eighty nine pounds of tobacco of the Defendants Estate
which he is ordered to pay to the Plantifs towards satisfying their Debt & costs
        - BENJAMIN HUBBARD Plt. against THOMAS WEST Deft.   On Attachment
CHARLES WEST, the Garnishee in this suit, being sworn & examined declared that he as
Executor of RICHARD WEST deced., should have (when he could make sale of the Testa-
tors Estate and receive the money arising thereby) sufficient in his hands to satisfy the
Plantif his demand, and thes aid Defendant being solemnly called failed to appear &
replevy the same. It is considered by the Court that the Plantif recover against the said
Defendant two pounds five shillings and ten pence, the Debt in the Attachment specified, also his costs in this behalf expended, and the said Defendant in Mercy &c., It is
ordered the Garnishee out of the money in his hands satisfy the Plantif his debt & costs

p.   Caroline County Court 8th of October 1772
148   - The Exor. of JOHN PRICE Gent., deced., Plt. against JOHN THILMAN, ROBERT
        MICKLEBERRY & JAS: HEAD LYNCH, Defts.   Motion on Replevy Bond
The Defendants who had legal notice of this motion being solemnly called failed to
appear; On motion of the Plantifs by their Attorney, Judgment is granted them against
the said Defendant for one hundred & thirty eight pounds twelve shillings, the Penalty
in the said Bond, to be discharged by the payment of Sixty four pounds six shillings
with legal Interest from the tenth day of June 1772 til paid & the costs of this motion
        - ROBINSON DANGERFIELD, Assee: of JOHN JONES, Plt. against JOHN THILMAN &
WILLIAM SOUTHWORTH, Defendts.   Motion on Replevy Bond   The Defendants who
had legal notice of this motion, being solemnly called failed to appear; On motion of the
Plantif by his Attorney, Judgment is granted him against the said Defendant for one
hundred & nineteen pounds five shillings & four pence, the Penalty in the said Bond to
be discharged by the payment of Fifty nine pounds twelve shillings and eight pence,
with legal Interest from the tenth day of June1772 til paid, & costs of this motion
        - ROBERT SCOTT Plt. against THOMAS BURK Deft.   Motion on Replevy Bond
The Defendant who had legal notice of this motion being solemnly called failed to
appear; On motion of the Plantif by his Attorney, Judgment is granted him against the
said Defendant for Seventeen pounds eight shillings & two pence, the Penalty in the
said Bond, to be discharged by the payment of Eighty pounds fourteen shillings & one
penny with legal Interest from the 22nd day of June 1772, til paid & costs of this motion

p.   Caroline County Court 8th of October 1772
149   - ANN TAYLOR Plt. against THOMAS BURK Deft. Motion on Replevy Bond
        The Defendant who had legal notice of this motion being solemnly called failed

to appear; On motion of the Plantif by her Attorney, Judgment is granted her against the said Defendant for five pounds seven shillings & two pence, the Penalty in the said Bond, to be discharged by the payment of Two pounds eighteen shillings & seven pence with legal Interest from the twenty second day of June 1772 til paid & costs of this motion

    - PHILLIP JOHNSTON Esqr., Assee: of JAMES TAYLOR Gent., Plt. against WILLIAM DUDLEY, GEORGE GUY, JEREMIAH RAWLINS, NATHANIEL NORMENT & EDMUND JONES Defendants. Motion of Replevy Bond   The Defendants who had legal notice of this motion being solemnly called failed to appear, On motion of the Plantif by his Attorney, Judgment is granted him against the said Defendants for One hundred and ten pounds two pence, the Penalty in the said Bond, to be discharged by the payment of Fifty five pounds & one penny with legal Interest from the tenth day of June 1772 til paid, & costs of this motion

    - WILLIAM STEVENS Plt. against JOHN MELONE, RICHARD JOHNSTON & JNO: GOODRICH, Defts.   Motion on a Replevy Bond   The Defendants who had legal notice of this motion, being solemnly called failed to appear. On motion of the Plantif by his Attorney, Judgment is granted him against the said Defendants for twelve pounds fourteen shillings and four pence, the Penalty in the said Bond, to be discharged by the payment of Six pounds seven shillings & two pence with legal Interest from the twentieth day of January 1772 til paid, & costs of this motion

    - Order'd WILLIAM JOHNSTON pay RICHARD ROY three hundred pounds of tobacco for attending this Court twelve days as an Evidence for him against ROY

p.   Caroline County Court 8th of October 1772
150   - Ordered the Sherif summon twenty four Freeholders of this County not being
    Ordinary Keepers, Constables, Surveyors of Highways, Owners of Mills or Occupiers thereof, to appear at the next Court that out of lthem a Grand Jury may be impannelled & sworn according to Law

    - JOHN HEWITT Plt. against JOHN PENN Deft.   In Case
Came the parties by their Attorneys, and thereupon came also a Jury, to wit, JNO: BROADDUS foreman &c., who were impannelled and sworn well & truly to try the matter on issue joined, do day that the Plantif hath sustained damages by reason of the said Defendant to twelve pounds four shillings & ten pence currt. money, But this Court being of the opinion that the damages are excessive, on motion of the Defendant a new trial is awarded him

    - MELCHESEDECK BRAME & RICHARD WYATT, Exors. of WALTER CHILES deced., Plts. against JAMES HEAD LYNCH Defendt.   In Debt   JOHN THILMAN entered himself Special Bail for the Defendant according to Law

    - WILLIAM MITCHELL, Assee. of JAMES LYLE, Plt. against JOHN HARRIS Deft., In Debt   HENRY ARMISTEAD entered himself Special Bail for the Defendant according to Law

    - WILLIAM BLADES Plt. against JOHN THILMAN Deft. In Debt
WM. SUTTON entered himself Special Bail for the Defendant according to Law

    - Messrs. DUNLOPs & CROSSE Plts. against WILLIAM BROWN JR. Deft. In Debt
ROBERT CHANDLER entered himself Special Bail for the Defendant according to Law

p.   Caroline County Court 8th of October 1772
151   - Ordered JOHN HEWETT pay CHELSON WHITE twenty five pounds of tobacco for
    attending this Court one day as an Evidence for him against JNO: PENN Gent.
    - Ordered JOHN HEWETT pay WM. DEW eighty five pounds of tobacco for attending

this Court one day and coming and returning twenty miles as an evidence for him against JNO: PENN Gent.

- Ordered JOHN HEWETT pay HUMPHREY BURETT twenty five pounds of tobacco for attending this Court one day as an evidence for him against JNO: PENN, Gent., and not to be taxed in Bill of costs

- The Inspectors at CONWAYS WAREHOUSE returned an Account of Tobacco in their hands amounting to Nineteen hundred & eighty four which they were directed to sell & they have returned that they sold the same for fourteen shillings & two pence p hundred

- SAML: PARTLOW is appointed Constable of the District from SOUTH RIVER up the South Branch to the SPOTSYLVANIA. It is ordered that he go before a Justice & be sworn according to Law

- Ordered that AQUILLA JOHNSTON, JOHN ESTIS, GEORGE YATES & ANDREW MUN-ROW, or any two of them, settle with ELIZA: REYNOLDS, her Administratrix Account of the Estate of JOSEPH REYNOLDS deced., and that they assign to the said ELIZABETH her thirds of the said Decedants Estate in this County; & it is ordered that RICHARD THOMAS, JNO: WRIGHT, ROBERT LANCASTER & WM. HALEY or any three of them allott to the said ELIZABETH REYNOLDS her third part of the said JOSEPH REYNOLDS Estate in ORANGE and that they make report thereof to Court

- Ordered JNO: THORNTON, WILLIAM WOODFORD & JNO: BUCKNER Gent., view the Warehouses at CONWAYS INSPECTION and Report to Court what proportion of Rent there should be between the Proprietor & County the last year & this year.

- JOHN HEWETT Plt. against JNO: PENN Gent. Deft.   In Case

p.   Caroline County Court 8th of October 1772
152   On motion of the Defendant by his Attorney, a Commission is awarded him to take the Deposition of HENRY LYNE & GEORGE GOBURN de bene esse giving the Plantif legal notice of the time & place appointed for taking the same

- Ordered that the Court be adjourn'd til the Court in Course

- The Minutes of the preceeding Orders were signed by
                                        ROBERT GILCHRIST, Gent.

(The remainder of this page is blank.)

p.   At a Court held for Caroline County on Thursday the Twelfth day of November
153   one thousand seven hundred and seventy two
                        Present His Majestys Justices
            EDMUND PENDLETON   WALKER TALIAFERRO
            ANTHONY THORNTON   SAMUEL HAWES
            JAMES MILLER   JAMES UPSHAW   Gentlemen
            JOHN BUCKNER   GEORGE GUY
            THOMAS LOWRY   ROGER QUARLES

- WEARS & WATSON against WILLIAM SUTTON   On Petition
Pursuant to an award made and returned by PAUL THILMAN, Gent., It is considered by the Court that the Petitioners recover against the said Defendant four pounds three shillings & six pence half penny, the Debt in the award mentioned, also their costs in this behalf expended

- RICHARD DICKENS Plt. against THOMAS COLLINS JR., Deft. Assault & Battery Dismissed, agreed

- A Commission & Certificate of Mrs. TAYLORs acknowledgment of a Deed from
herself & Husband to MASON returned and ordered to be recorded
- MESS PICKETT Plt. against DANIEL BARKSDALE Deft.   In Case
Pursuant to an award made & returned by JAMES TAYLOR, RICHARD JOHNSTON &
JAMES JOHNSTON, It is considered by the Court that the Plantif recover against the said
Defendant Twelve pounds ten shillings & eleven pence, the Debt in the award specified

p.   Caroline Count Court 12th of November 1772
154   - Ordered the Clerk add four Tithes belonging to SAMUEL RAWLINS to the List
of JAMES MILLER Gent.
- A Sale & Division of the Estate of JNO: COMER deced., returned & ordered to be
recorded
- On motion of ANN FOX, (who having taken the Oath prescribed by Law) Certificate for obtaining Letters of Administration on the Estate of WM: FOX deced., is granted
her, Bond acknowledged & ordered to be recorded
- Ordered ROBERT GILCHRIST, ANDREW LECKIE, JAMES DUNLOP & JAMES BOWIE
JR., Gent., or any three of them (being first sworn) do appraise the Estate of WM: FOX
deced. according to Law
- THOMAS LOWRY & JAMES UPSHAW Gent., are appointed to view the the Commissioners appointed by KING & QUEEN Court,MARROCOCICK BRIDGE and report to Court the
value thereof
- A Deed Poll from ELIZABETH PEAY to MARTHA NODEN proved by the witnesses
& ordered to be recorded
- A Deed Indented from WM: MASON & MARY his Wife (she being first privately
examined) to SAML: BURRUS acknowledged & ordered to be recorded
- A Deed Indented from FREDERICK FORTSON to STEPHEN FORTSON further proved
by the Oaths of JNO: ALEXR: STILL & AQUILLA TIGNOR & ordered to be recorded
- A Deed Indented from JAMES FARISH & FANNY his Wife (she being first privately examined) to THOMAS COLEMAN SENR., acknowledged & ordered to be recorded
- An Inventory & Appraisment of the Estate of CHARLES BEAZLEY deced.,
return'd & ordered to be recorded
- ELIZABETH JOHNSTON is appointed, on motion of DANIEL & CLARA JOHNSONs, to
be their Guardian, Bond acknowledged & ordered to be recorded
- Ordered GEORGE GUY, JEREMIAH RAWLINS, NATHL: NORMENT & JNO: BAYNHAM
or any three of them divide the Estate of RICHD: WEST deced. among his Legatees agreeable to his Will
- An Inventory & Appraisement of the Estate of JOSEPH GAUNT deced., return'd
& ordered to be recorded

p.   Caroline County Court 12th of November 1772
155   - The Nuncupative Will of RICHARD WOOLFOLK CHANDLER proved by the Oaths
of SAML: WORTHAM, NATHL: YOUNG & REUBEN GEORGE & ordered to be recorded;
On motion of JOSEPH RICHESON & ROBT. CHANDLER (who having taken the Oath pre-
scribed by Law) Certificate for obtaining a Probate thereof is granted them, Bond ack-
nowledged, & ordered to be recorded
- Ordered ROBERT MICKLEBERRY, NORMENT DICKEN, THOMAS DICKENSON &
REUBEN GEORGE, or any three of them (being first sworn) appraise that part of the
Estate of RICHD: WOOLFOLK CHANDLER deced., being in HANOVER County according to
Law.

- WILLIAM BUCKNER made choice of JNO: BUCKNER Gent., to be his Guardian, Bond acknowledged & ordered to be recorded
- ELIZABETH BUCKNER made choice of GEORGE BUCKNER to be his Guardian, Bond acknowledged & ordered to be recorded
- On motion of BENJAMIN SNEED leave is granted him to keep an ORDINARY at his Father's House in this County
- ANTHONY THORNTON, CHARLES ROBINSON, HARRY BEVERLEY & ANTHONY THORNTON JR., Gent. or any three of them are appointed to divide the Estate of THOMAS BUCKNER Gent., deced., agreeable to his Will, & ELIZABETH BUCKNER, Mother of the Infant Children, is appointed Guardian of them to act in the division
- SAMUEL HAWES & GEORGE YATES are added to those appointed to appraise the Estate on MATTAPONY of THOMAS BUCKNER deced.
- Ordered ROBERT GILCHRIST, JAMES TAYLOR, JNO: BUCKNER & CHARLES ROBINSON Gent., or any three of them divide the Estate of GEORGE KENNER deced., agreeable to his Will & that they settle the Account of Administration of the Decedants Estate
- A Deed Indented from WALKER &c. to FITZHUGH further proved by the Oath of GEORGE ISBELL & ordered to be recorded
- WALKER TALIAFERRO, JNO: PENN, SAML: HAWES & BENJAMIN TOMPKINS, or any three of them, are appointed to settle with the Executors of JOSEPH WOOLFOLK deced. their Account of Executorship of the Decedants Estate

p.   Caroline County Court 12th of November 1772
156   - A Deed Indented from NICHS: QUISENBERRY to HACKETT proved by the Oath of RICHARD DIXON & ordered to be recorded
- On motion of FRANCIS THORNTON, Security for DANL: LOVELL, Exr. of JACOB LOVELL deced., and the Defendant appearing in Court, It is ordered he give counter security or deliver up the Decedants Estate
- A Mortgage from WM: BROWN JR. to ROBERT CHANDLER further proved & ordered to be recorded
- An Assignment of a Bill of Sale from JOSHUA GRADY to MARGARET YOUNG and from said YOUNG to CATESBY YOUNG, acknowledged & ordered to be recorded
- Ordered MESS PICKETT pay WILLIAM PICKETT Two hundred pounds of tobacco for attending this Court eight days as an evidence for him against DANIEL BARKSDALE
- ANDREW MONROE is appointed Overseer of the Road in the room of THOMAS SCOTT
- GEORGE ATKISON Plt. against JOHN MITCHELL Deft.   In Debt ANTHONY THORNTON JR., Gent., entered himself Special Bail for the Defendant according to Law
- Ordered JNO: HEWETT pay CHELSON WHITE twenty five pounds of tobacco for attending this Court one day as an evidence for him against JNO: PENN Gent.
- Ordered JNO: HEWETT pay WILLIAM DEW Eighty five pounds of tobacco for attending this Court one day & once coming & returning twenty miles as an evidence for him against JNO: PENN Gent.
- THOMAS LOWRY & JAMES UPSHAW Gent. are appointed to settle the Executorship of ELIAS BLACKBURN deced. Estate with the Administrator
- BENJAMIN TOMPKINS is appointed Overseer of the Road in the room of JNO: DURRETT
- EDMUND PENDLETON, JAMES UPSHAW & THOMAS ROANE Gent., are appointed by consent of THOMAS DAVIS & WM. SPINDLE, Guardian of ELIZABETH DAVIS to finally settle & divide the Estate of EDWARD & LETITIA DAVIS & report to Court

p   Caroline County Court 12th of November 1772
157   -- ROBERT HART Complt. against WILLIAM DUDLEY, Defendt.   In Chancery
        On motion of the Defendant by his Attorney, further time is allowed for the
Referees to make their report and it is agreed that if either party fails to attend at the
time & place appointed for settling their Accounts, that the Referees proceed without
the part so failing provided he has legal notice thereof if after the Complainant shall
have furnished the Defendant with a Copy of his Account, sicne the Judgment of
HANOVER COURT against the said Defendant
        - JAMES BEADLES Plt. against THOMAS WEST Deft.   On Attachment
CHARLES WEST, the Garnishee in this suit, being sworn & examined, declared that he as
Executor of his Father, RICHD. WEST deced., shall have in his hands a Legacy of Ten
pounds given the said THOMAS by the Will of the said Testator out of which he has
assumed to pay a demand of BENJA: HUBBARD; And the said Defendant being solemnly
called failed to appear & replevy the same; It is considered by the Court that the Plantif
recover against the said Defendant One pound eleven shillings & two pence, the Debt in
the Attachment specified; also his costs in this behalf expended; & the said Defendant in
Mercy &c., It is ordered that the Garnishee after satisfying the demand of BENJAMIN
HUBBARD pay the Plantif his Debt & costs if sufficient in his hands
        - JOHN ELLIOT PAYNE against THOMAS WEST   On Attachment
CHARLES WEST, the Garnishee in this suit, being sworn & examined, declared that he as
Executor of his Father, RICHD: WEST deced., shall have in his hands a Legacy of Ten
pounds given the said THOS: by the Will of the said Testator, out of which he has
assumed to pay a demand of BENJAMIN HUBBARD; And the said Defendant being solemnly called failed to appear & replevy the same

p.   Caroline County Court 12th of November 1772
158   It is ordered by the Court that the Plantif recover against the said Defendant
        One pound ten shillings, the Debt in the Attachment specified; also his costs in
this behalf expended, And the said Defendant in Mercy &c., It is ordered that the Garnishee after satisfying BENJA: HUBBARD & JAMES BEADLES, their demand, pay the
Plantif his Debt & costs if sufficient in his hands
        - JOHN CUMMIN Plt. against JAMES PATTIE Deft. Case for Slander
Pursuant to an award made & returned by EDWD. DIXON, ANDREW LECKIE & JNO:
SKINKER, It is considered by the Court that the Plantif recover against the said Defendant Two pounds thirteen shillings & ten pence, the Debt in the award mentioned; also
his costs in this behalf expended and the said Defendt. in Mercy &c.
        - JOHN CUMMIN Plt. against JAMES PATTIE Deft.   Assault & Battery
Pursuant to an award made & returned by EDWARD DIXON, ANDREW LECKIE & JNO:
SKINKER, It is considered by the Court that the same be dismissed and that each party
pay their costs in this matter expended
        - JAMES PATTIE Plt. against JOHN CUMMINS Deft.   In Case
Pursuant to an award made & returned by EDWARD DIXON, ANDREW LECKIE & JNO:
SKINKER, It is considered by the Court that the Plantif recover against the said Defen-
dant two pounds thirteen shillings & ten pence, the Debt in the award specified, also his
costs in this behalf expended
        - JAMES BOWIE JR. against JAMES CHARLES   On Attachment
On motion of the Plantif, ordered the Clerk redockett this Attachment

p.   Caroline County Court 12th of November 1772
159   - SAMUEL RICHARDS, ISRAEL MANDETT & COMPY. Assignees of BOHANNON &
        HAMILTON Complaints. against JAMES LEDFORD, AMBROSE VAUGHN & MARY

his Wife, JOHN LEDFORD, JAMES LOVING & SALLY his Wife, HENRY MARTIN & ANN his Wife, JOSEPH LEDFORD & AUGUSTINE VAUGHN & CATY his Wife & POLLY LEDGORD, Defendants In Chancery The Commissioners who were appointed to report who were in possession of the slaves in the Bill mentioned and their increase, have reported that the Defendants AMBROSE VAUGHN, JNO: LEDFORD & JAMES LOVING have them in their possession; Therefore it is decreed & ordered that THOMAS LOWRY, JAMES UPSHAW & EDMUND PENDLETON JR., Gent., or any two of them, make sale of so many of the slaves & their increase in the Bill mentioned as will be sufficient to satisfy the Complainants their Decree and costs

    - MESS PICKETT Complt. against WILLIAM HARRISON &c., Defts. In Chancery On motion of the Defendant by his Council, a Commission is awarded him to take the Deposition of JOHN GRIFFIS, who it is alledged is about to leave the Colony

    - GEORGE ATKISON Plt. against JOHN MITCHELL Deft. In Debt HARRY BEVERLEY, who was security for the Defendants appearance, produced the Defendant in Court in discharge of his recognizance & the Plantif moved that he might be ruled to give Special Bail. Whereupon the Defendant made default. On motion of the said Plantif by his Attorney, it is ordered that the Defendant be & remain in Custody of the Sherif until he be legally discharged and the said Defendant prays leave til next Court to consider of & answer the Plantifs Writ & Declaration which is granted him

p.   Caroline County Court 12th of November 1772
160   - HAMPTON RALL Plt. against EDWARD STEVENS, Deft. On Petition for Freedom
    Came the Plantif by his Attorney & a Commission is awarded him to take the Deposition of MARIA MULLIN debe ne esse, who it is said is infirm

    - WILLIAM NELSON, Assignee of JOHN JONES Plt. against WILLIAM BROWN JR. & GARROTT HACKETT, Defts. Motion on Replevy Bond
The Defendants who had legal notice of this motion being solemnly called failed to appear; On motion of the Plantif by his Attorney, Judgment is granted him against the said defendants for Forty pounds currt. money the Penalty of the said Bond; to be discharged by the payment of Nineteen pounds fifteen shillings & eleven pence with legal Interest from the fifteenth day of July one thousand seven hundred and seventy two til paid & costs of this motion

    - PHILLIP MOUNTAGUE, Exor. of WILLIAM ROANE deced., Plt. against DANIEL HAYES & DANIEL TURNER Defts. Motion on Replevy Bond
The Defendants who had legal notice of this motion, being solemnly called failed to apper, On motion of the Plantif by his Attorney, Judgment is granted him against the said Defendants for ten pounds eight shillings & two pence, the Penalty of said Bond, to be discharged by the payment of five pounds four shillings & one penny with legal Interest from the seventeenth day of July 1772 til paid & costs of this motion

    - A GRAND JURY for the body of this County being impanelled & sworn received their charge, withdrew, & in a short time returned their Presentments as follows;
    "We the GRAND JURY present JACOB BURRUS for not keeping his Mill Dam in repair

p.   Caroline County Court 12th of November 1772
161   according to Law;
    ANDREW ROSS, THOMAS KELLEY & MATTHEW GALE for disobeying the Legal commands of ANTHY: THORNTON Gent.
    RICHARD WOOLFOLK CHANDLER for concealing one Tythe; JOHN YOUNG for the same; JOHN SMITH for the same; JOHN LUCAS for concealing two tythes,
    WILLIAM GOODALL for not giving in his list of Tithables;

RICHARD MICOU for concealing two wheels; JOHN ARMISTEAD Gent. for the same; CHITWOOD PARR for not giving in his List of Tythes;

ANTHONY NEW Gent., for concealing one tythe; RICHARD ROY for concealing two wheels; THOMAS ROYSTON for concealing two wheels,, BENJAMIN HUBBARD for concealing one tythe; ELIZABETH FORTUNE for the same;

                                        ROBERT   MICKLEBERRY, foreman
Ordered that the several Offenders be summoned to appear at the next Court to answer thereto

- For reasons appearing to the Court, It is ordered that JOHN HAMPTON, PHILLIP ESTIS & WM: HEWLETT in conjunction with JOHN MINOR Gent., THOMAS TERRIL, JOHN CHILES & ROBERT (blank) or any three of them, being first sworn, view the way petitioned for by WILLIAM McGHEE, &c. & report to Court the conveniences and inconveniences attending the same

- Ordered that the Court be adjourned til the Court in Course
- The Minutes of the preceeding Orders were signed by
                                        JOHN BUCKNER Gent.

p.   At a Court held for Caroline County the Tenth day of December one thousand
162   seven hundred and seventy two
                        Present His Majestys Justices
            ROBERT GILCHRIST   ANTHONY THORNTON
            WALKER TALIAFERRO   JOHN BUCKNER &   Gent.
            JAMES MILLER   ROGER QUARLES

	Tobo:	
- The Court proceeded to lay the County Levy		
To the Kings Attorney his Salary	2080	
To the Clerks salary	1248	
To the Sherif for Extraordinary services	1248	
To Mr. Secretary, his Account	610	
To BENJAMIN TOMPKINS for Building three Bridges per Account when received		L. 44..9
To CHILSON WHITE for setting up a Sign Post	50	
To SAMUEL CURL his Account for Guarding Negro Abraham	150	
To JOHN REYNOLDS for the same service	150	
To JEDDIAH JOHNSTON for the same service	150	
To GEORGE EUBANK for the same service	150	
To WILLIAM LUCAS for building a Bridge over (B---) SWAMP & assigned to		
HENRY CRUTCHFIELD	250	
To the Sherif per Account	870	
To JOHN WILY JUNR. for setting up three Sign Posts	150	
To JOHN WILY SENR. assigned to JAMES MILLER for keeping BURKS BRIDGE		L. 5
	7106	L 49..9

- Present JOHN MINOR, Gent.
- For reasons appearing to the Court, BENJAMIN HUBBARD is excused from the Presentment of the GRAND JURY found against him for concealing one tythe
- For reasons appearing to the Court, THOMAS ROYSTON, RICHARD ROY & RICHARD MICOU are excused from the Presentment of the GRAND JURY found against them for concealing two wheels
- For reasons appearing to the Court, CHITWOOD PARR is excused from the Presentment of the GRAND JURY found against him for concealing his tythes. It is ordered the Clerk add two Tithables belonging to the said PARR to the List taken by JAMES MILLER Gent.

- Present SAMUEL HAWES, Gent.

p.   Caroline County Court 10th of December 1772
163   - On motion of JOHN BEVERLEY ROY, who having taken the Oath prescribed by
        Law, Certificate for obtaining Letters of Administration of the Estate of THOMAS
ROY deceased is granted him, Bond acknowledged & ordered to be recorded
        - On motion of ROBERT GILCHRIST & ANDREW LECKIE Gent., who having taken
the Oath prescribed by Law, Certificate for obtaining Letters of Administration on the
Estate of JAMES SULLINGER deceased is granted them, Bond acknowledged & ordered to
be recorded
        - Ordered ROBERT GILCHRIST Gent., JOHN CATLETT, ANDREW LECKIE & JAMES
DUNLOP or any three of them being first sworn appraise the Estate of THOMAS ROY deceased according to Law
        - Ordered GILES NEWTON, ROBERT KAY, JAMES KAY & JOHN LONG or any three of
them being first sworn appraise the Estate of JAMES SULLINGER deceased according to
Law
        - For reasons assigned to the Court, ANTHONY NEW Gent., is excused from the
Presentment of the GRAND JURY found against him for concealing one Tythe
        - JOHN LUCAS, for reasons appearing to the Court, is discharged from the Pre-
sentment of the GRAND JURY, found against him for concealing one Tythe
        - For reasons assigned to the Court, EDMUND LUCAS is discharged from the
County Levy
        - On motion of WILLIAM BUCKNER, leave is granted him to keep an ORDINARY at
his Hosue on his giving Bond & Security in the Clerks Office
        - Our Sovereign Lord the King against JACOB BURRUS   Presentment
 For reasons assigned & the Defendant having promised to open the Old Road near his
Mill. he is excused from the Presentment of the GRAND JURY, & It is considered by the
Court that the Plantif recover against the said Defendant his costs by him in this behalf
expended
        - JOSEPH RICHESON is appointed Guardian to TIMOTHY CHANDLER, Bond acknow-
ledged & ordered to be recorded
        - Ordered JOSEPH CAVELL, HUGH ROSE, CHARLES ROSE & DANIEL GAINES Gent., or
any two of them, divide the Estate of WILLIAM CROUCHER deceased, agreeable to his Will
& report to this Court
        - Ordered that JAMES UPSHAW, WILLIAM LYNE & JOHN RICHARDS Gent. or any
two of them settle with JOHN ELLIOT PAYNE his Administration Account of LEDFORDs
Estate

p.   Caroline County Court 10th of December 1772
164   - JAMES JOHNSTON Plt. against DAVID & PEYTON STERNs Defts. Motion on
        Replevy Bond   The Defendants who had legal notice of this miton being
solemnly called failed to appear, On motion of the Plantif by his Attorney, Judgment is
granted against him the said Defendant for Eight pounds fifteen shilllings; the Penalty
of the said Bond; to be discharged by the payment of four pounds eleven shillings &
eleven pence with legal Interest from the Tenth day of August one thousand seven
hundred & seventy two til paid and the costs of this motion
        - A Deed Indented from WILLIAM TOOMBS & MARY his Wife to THOMAS SHIP
JUNR. she being first privately examined, acknowledged by her & proved by two
witnesses as to TOOMBS & ordered to be recorded

- Ordered JOHN HEWETT pay LARKIN DULING Two hundred & twenty five pounds
of tobacco for attending this Court five days & twice coming & returning twenty miles
as an evidence for him agst. JOHN PENN, Gent.
- Present ANTHONY NEWGENT, Gent.
- HAMPTON RALL against EDWARD STEVENS   Petition for Freedom
Came the parties by their Attorneys, & on motion of the Petitioner, a Commission is
awarded him to take the Deposition of MARGARET YOUNG & JOHN ROBINSON de bene esse
giving legal notice of the time & place appointed for taking the same
- RICHARD GOODALL Plt. against ROBERT MICKLEBERRY Deft.   In Case
On motion of the Defendant by his Attorney, a Commission is awarded him to take the
Deposition of GEORGE WILLIAMSON who resides out of this Colony
- Ordered the Court be adjourned til the Court in Course
- The Minutes of the preceeding Orders were signed by
                                    WALKER TALIAFERRO, Gent.

p.   At a Court held for Caroline County on Thursday the Eleventh day of February
165   one thousand seven hundred and seventy three
                        Present His Majestys Justices
            EDMUND PENDLETON   THOMAS LOWRY
            ANTHONY THORNTON   JAMES UPSHAW   Gent.
            WALKER TALIAFERRO   JAMES ARMISTEAD

- JAMES GOVAN Plantif against HUMPHREY HALEY Defendt.   In Case
Came the Plantif by his Attorney & the Defendant by Note from under his hand agrees
that Judgment should be entered against him for Eleven pounds seven shillings & four
pence; Therefore it is considered by the Court that the Plantif recover against the said
Defendant the said sum of Eleven pounds seven shillings & four pence by the Defendant
in manner & form aforesaid confessed; also his costs in this behalf expended & the said
Defendant in Mercy &c.
- HART & MARSHALL Plts. against WALTER MACKIE, Surviving Obligor of JOHN
MACKIE deced. Defendt.   In Debt   Came the Plantifs by their Attorney & the
Defendant in his proper person & the said Defendant saith he cannot deny the Plantifs
action, Therefore it is considered by the Court that the Plantifs recover against the said
Defendant One hundred twenty three pounds five shillings & eleven pence half penny,
the Debt in the Declaration mentioned; also their costs in this behalf expended & the
said Defendant in Mercy &c., This Judgment except the costs is to be discharged by the
payment of Sixty one pounds twelve shillings & eleven pence three farthings with
legal Interest from the Ninth day of October one thousand seven hundred & seventy two
til paid
- JAMES WARE SENR. is appointed Guardian of ELIZABETH & AGNIS HURT,
Orphans of JAMES HURT deced., Bond acknowledged & ordered to be recorded

p.   Caroline County Court 11th of February 1773
166   - On motion of BENJAMIN LAHONE by WILLIAM BOWLER his Attorney, Judg-
        ment is granted him against EDMUND TAYLOR, Deputy Sherif of HANOVER, for
two pounds for failing to return an Execution he recovered against RICHARD GOODALL
- The Will of ELIZABETH WALDEN deced., was proved by the witnesses and
ordered to be recorded; On motion of JNO: WALDEN (who having made Oath presecribed
by Law) Certificate for obtaining a Probate thereof is granted him; Bond acknowledged
and ordered to be recorded

- A Deed Indented from JOHN MINTER &c. to ANTHONY MINTER proved by the Oaths of JNO: & JOSEPH WINTER & ordered to be recorded

- On motion of BENJAMIN HURT & JNO: YOUNG, ordered JNO: SUTTON, NATHANIEL NORMENT & SAMUEL BURRUS or any two of them divide the Estate of TITUS HURT deced agreeable to his Will

- The Will of ADAM MERRYMAN deced. was proved by the Oaths of GEORGE & JAMES STONEHAM & ordered to be recorded; On motion of the Executrix therein named; Certificate for obtaining a Probate thereof is granted her, Oath administred, Bond acknowledged & ordered to be recorded

- Ordered SETH THORNTON, FRANCIS TALIAFERRO, DAVID CHEVIS & GEORGE TURNER or any three of them (being first sworn) do appraise the Estate of ADAM MERRIMAN deced., according to Law

- Ordered the Treasurer of this County pay SAMUEL HARGROVE the further sum of Seven pounds ten shillings as the proportion of this County for building and maintaining the Bridge across PAMUNKEY RIVER from the Eleventh day of November last for seven years to come

- Ordered to be certified to the Treasurer of this Colony that ROBERT GILCHRIST Gent , by Order of this Court hath imported a Scale Beam for the use of ROYS WAREHOUSE and Weights to the amount of Twenty seven pounds thirteen shillings & seven pence half penny

- Ordered that ROBERT GILCHRIST & JAMES MILLER Gent., agree with some workmen to repair or rebuild the Bridge across PEWMANSEND below RAWLINS's

p   Caroline County Court 11th of February 1773
167   - A Deed Indented from HARRY TALIAFERRO & Wife to THOS: CATLETT proved by
         the Oaths of two witnesses & ordered to be certified, & a Commission of Mrs.
TALIAFERRO's acknowledgment returned & ordered to be recorded

- A Deed Indented from BENJA: BAUGHAN & DOROTHY his Wife (she being first privately examined) to WM: YOUNG acknowledged and ordered to be recorded

- A Deed Indented from JNO: TAYLOR to BENJAMIN CATLETT was proved by the witnesses & ordered to be recorded

- A Deed Indented from THOS: CATLETT to LEWIS JONES was proved by two witnesses & ordered to be certified

- CATY JOHNSTON made choice of ROBERT COLEMAN to be her Guardian; Bond acknowledged & ordered to be recorded

- A Bill of Sale from WM: TOOMBS to JNO: GRIFFIN proved by the witnesses & ordered to be recorded

- Absent EDMUND PENDLETOIN Gent. & ANTHONY THORNTON Gent.

- Present JAMES TAYLOR, ROBERT GILCHRIST, SAMUEL HAWES, GEORGE GUY & ROGER QUARLES Gent.

- A Deed Poll from JNO: NORMENT to WM: SUTTON proved by the witnesses & ordered to be recorded

- A Deed Poll from CHARLES PEMBERTON to DELPHIA GARNETT proved by the witnesses & ordered to be recorded

- An Inventory & Appraisement of the Estate of LARKIN GARNETT deced., returned & ordered to be recorded

- A Deed Indented from JAMES POWELL to MESS PICKETT proved by the witnesses & ordered to be recorded

- The Will of JNO: WINTERTON was proved by the Oaths of ROBERT GILCHRIST Gent., JNO: BRAND & ROBERT PARKER and ordered to be recorded On motion of ELIZA-

BETH ATKINS, the Exrx. therein named (who having taken the Oath prescribed by Law) Certificate for obtaining a Probate thereof is granted her, Bond acknowledged & ordered to be recorded

    - Ordered JNO: BROWN, JNO: BRAND, EDWARD POWERS & JNO: CUMMIN or any three of them (being first sworn) do appraise the Estate of JNO: WINTERTON deced., according to Law

p.   Caroline County Court 11th of February 1773
168   - On motion of NATHANIEL NORMENT, leave is granted him to keep an ORDI-NARY at his House near the REEDY MILL

    - HENRY LYNE JUNR. against ROBERT WOOLFOLK & JOHN WOOLFOLK   Motion on Replevy Bond   the Defendants who had legal notice of this motion being solemnly called failed to appear; On motion of the Plantif by his Attorney, Judgment is granted him against the said Defendants for Seven pounds three shillings current money to be discharged by the payment of three pounds eleven shillings & six pence with legal Interest from the fourth day of July 1772 til paid; & costs of this motion

    - Ordered ANTHONY NEW Gent., THOMAS DICKENSON & REUBEN GEORGE lor any two of them settle that part of the Estate of JNO: WHITLOCK deced. to which ELIZABETH, his Daughter, is Intituled to and in order to raise such part, ordered that they sell one of the slaves of the Decedant and the Surplus to be accounted for by the Administrator

    - NICHOLAS WARE JUNR. against JNO: PLANT & JNO: GEORGE hhd. Motion on Replevy Bond   The Defendant who had legal notice of this motion being solemnly called failed to appear; On motion of the Plantif by his Attorney, Judgment is granted him against the said Defendant for Five pounds four shillings, the Penalty of the said Bond, to be discharged by the payment of Two pounds twelve shillings with legal Interest from the Thirtieth day of July one thousand seven hundred & seventy two till paid & costs of this motion

    - GEORGE TURNER is appointed Overseer of the Road in the room of BENJAMIN ALLSOP

p.   Caroline County Court 11th of February 1773
169   - ISAAC HAWES against RICHARD CONQUEST & HENRY PEMBERTON   Motion on Replevy Bond   The Defendants who had legal notice of this motion being solemnly called failed to appear; On motion of the Plantif by his Attorney, Judgment is granted him against the said Defendant for Eight punds one shilling & six pence, the Penalty in the said Bond, to be discharged by the payment of Four poudns and seven pence with legal interest from the 24th day of July one thousand seven hundred & seventy two til paid & costs of this motion

    - A Commission & Certificate of MRS. BROWNs acknowledgment of a Deed from her Husband & self to RICHD: GOODALL returned & ordered to be recorded

    - A Deed Indented from RICHARD GOODALL to WILLIAM CHILES proved by the Oaths of three witnesses & ordered to be recorded

    - HARRY CROUTCHER is appointed Overseer of the Road in the room of PETER THORNTON Gent.

    - CHARLES WEST is appointed Overseer of the Road from the REEDY MILL to BOOT SWAMP

    - On motion of ANTHONY THORNTON, Gent., for administration on the Estate of ELIZABETH McPHERSON deceased, the same being contested by CHARLES DICK Gent., in behalf of the Trustees & Feoffees of the Town of FREDERICKSBURG, On hearing the witnesses, exhibits & arguments of Counsel on both sides, the Court are of opinion that the said ANTHONY THORNTON Gent. (there appears to be more to this entry for the remainder of the page is blank)

p   Caroline County Court 11th of February 1773
170   - JAMES MILLER Gent., Plantif against WILLIAM TOOMBS Defendt.
On Attachment   This day came the Plantif by his Attorney and the Sherif made return that he levied the same on a Hogshead of tobacco at the Warehouse, a parcel of tobacco hanging in the House, a Feather bed &c., a Chest & Table, a Loom & Spinning Wheel, two chairs, iron pott & hooks, a stack of Tops, a parcel of Corn in the Field, narrow Ax, grubbing & weeding hoes, a Negroe, three head of Cattle and in the hands of THOS: SHIP JUNR., a sow & piggs, & one Shoat & a Hoggshead of tobacco found in GEORGE ALSOPs Plantation, And the said Defendant being solemnly called, failed to appear & replevy the same; Therefore it is considered by the Court that the Plantif recover against the said Defendant One hundred & thirteen pounds, ten shillings & two pence currt. money, the Debt in the said Attachment specified; Together with his costs in this behalf expended; & the said Defendant in Mercy &c., But this Judgment except the costs is to be discharged by the payment of fifty six pounds fifteen shillings & one penny with legal Interest from the seventh day of March one thousand seven hundred & seventy one til paid. JAMES DUNLOP appeared & claimed a right to the Hogshead of tobo: found in GEORGE ALSOPs Plantation. On hearing the Testimony offered; the Court are of opinion he has a right thereto. It is ordered that the Sherif make sale of the Estate by him attached (except the Negro & the other hogshead of tobacco) & pay the money arising thereby towards discharging this Judgment & the Attachment is continued to the Negro & tobo:
    - ROBERT HART Complainant against WILLIAM DUDLEY Defendant
In Chancery   The Defendant having failed to file his answer agreeable to the Rule of this Court and the Commissioners, who were appointed to adjust the ballance due the Complainant on the Mortgage in the Bill mentioned, having made their report; It is therefore ordered that the Complainant recover against the said Defendant One hundred & forty five pounds twelve shillings & eight pence currt. money with legal Interest on One hundred & twenty six pounds eighteen shillings & four pence from the nineteenth day of December one thousand seven hundred & seventy two til paid; toge- ther with his costs in this behalf expended; & it is also ordered that GEORGE GUY, JERE- MIAH RAWLINS & JOHN BAYNHAM Gent. or any two of them

p.   Caroline County Court 11th of February 1773
171   (if the Defendant fails to satisfy this Decree by the Twenty fifth day of April next) make sale of as much of the Mortgaged Land in the Bill mentioned at six months credit as will satisfy this Decree and the the Defendant be foreclosed of all Equity of Redemption in the land so to be sold
    - JOHN TURNER Plt against JOHN HARVEY Defendt.   In Debt
Pursuant to an award made & returned by GEORGE GUY, JERE: RALLINS & JOHN BAYN- HAM, It is considered by the Court that the Plantif recover against the said Defendant Ten pounds currt. money and also his costs in this behalf expended and the said Defen- dant in Mercy &c
    - THE COURT PROCEEDED to Conclude the County Levy

	L.	lbs. Tobo:
To Mr. WILLIAM NELSON by Account	9...8...0	200
To Mr. ROBERT GILCHRIST by Account	2.16...0	
To ANDREW ROSS by Account		12
To RICHARD JOHNSTON, Exr. of FRANCIS COLEMAN for EDWARD HERNDON & part of BARTHOLOMEW CHEWNING Prison Fees		807

To MRS. HANNAH COLEMAN her Account	3155
To Tobacco to be paid the Treasurer and by him sold to discharge the money claims	10885
To amount brought forward	7160
To the Sherif for collecting 23580	1415
	23580

                    Contra
By 4716 Tithables at Five pounds of Tobacco p. Poll   23580
    Ordered the Sherif collect of every Tithable person in this County five pounds of tobacco
        - On the Petition of JOHN BAYNHAM, Ordered GEORGE GUY, NATHANIEL NORMENT & JERE: RALLINS or any two of them being first sworn, view the way to be shewn them by JOHN BAYNHAM and report to Court
        - WILLIAM PEATROSS is appointed Overseer of the Road in the room of JOHNSON FAULKNER
        - It appearing to the Court that REMERS MANN is full age and by the consent of his Master, JOHN SUTTON, he is released from further service

p.   Caroline County Court 11th of February 1773
172   - Ordered that the Court be adjourned till the Court in Course
           - The Minutes of the preceeding Orders were signed by
                                        EDMUND PENDLETON, Gent.

        - At a Court held for Caroline County the Eleventh day of March one thousand
                seven hundred & seventy three
                    Present His Majestys Justices
            ANTHONY THORNTON   JOHN MINOR   &
            JAMES UPSHAW   ROGER QUARLES   Gentlemen

        - JAMES UPSHAW and BENJAMIN HUBBARD Gent., are added to the Gentlemen appointed to appraise the Estate of JNO: BAYLOR Esqr., deceased
        - A Deed Indented from NATHANIEL DICKERSON to (blank) DICKERSON acknowledged & ordered to be recorded
        - On motion of JOHN BAYLOR, who having taken the Oath prescribed by Law, Certificate for obtaining a Probate is granted him of the Will of JNO: BAYLOR Esqr. deceased, Bond acknowledged, & ordered to be recorded
        - SEYMOUR HOE took the usual Oaths to his Majestys person & Government, repeated & subscribed the Test, and was sworn as Practitioner of Law
        - JOHN HIPKINS, WILLIAM STRESHLY & RICHARD BUCKNER took the usual Oath to his Majestys person & Government, repeated & subscribed the Test, the sd: HIPKINS as Ensign, STRESHLY as Lieutenant & BUCKNER as Captain of Malitia
        - An Indenture of Apprenticeship between WHARTON & DILLIN read, approved of by the Court, and ordered to be recorded
        - A Deed Poll from YARBROUGH to WILKINSON proved by two witnesses & ordered to be recorded
        - A Deed Poll from ELIZABETH PEMBERTON to WM:, REUBEN, JOHN, AGNES & MOLLY PEMBERTON proved by three witnesses & ordered to be recorded
        - On motion of JOHN MICKLEBERRY, Attorney for WILLIAM GOODALL of the Province of GEORGIA, administration on the Estate of JAMES GOODALL deced. in this Colony is granted him; Oath administered, Bond acknowledged & ordered to be recorded

p.   Caroline County Court 11th of March 1773
173   - Ordered JOHN ROBINSON, JOHN LAWRENCE, JOHN HERNDON & THOMAS ANDER-
      SON or any three of them (being first sworn, do appraise the Estate of JAMES
GOODALL deceased according to Law
      - WILLIAM MURRAH is appointed Overseer of the Road from MARMAZOKE ROAD
to MOUNT CHURCH
      - RICHARD BUCKNER is appointed Overseer of the Road from the MOUNT HILL to
PROSSERS SWAMP
      - WILLIAM HEWLETT et Uxor Plts. against EUCLID WHITLOCK Deft.
  Assault & Battery   On motion of the Plantifs by their Attorney, a Commission is
awarded them to take the Deposition of ANN WHITLOCK de bene esse, giving legal notice
of the time & place appointed for taking the same
      - Ordered the hands of SUSANA TANKERSLEY work on the Road whereof THOMAS
SLAUGHTER is Overseer
      - ARCHD: McCALL & COMPY., Plts. against HENRY MARTIN & JNO: MARTIN & JNO:
LOVERN. Motion on Replevy Bond   The Defendants who had legal notice of this
motion being solemnly called failed to appear. On motion of the Plantif, Judgment is
granted him against the said Defendants for Eleven pounds fifteen shillings & eight
pence, the Penalty of the said Bond, to be discharged by the payment of Five pounds
seventeen shillings & ten pence with legal Interest from the 5th day of June one thousand seven hudnred & seventy two til paid & costs of this motion
      - Messrs. DUNLOPs & CROSSE Plts. against RICHARD MILEAR Deft.   In Case
Dismissed, agreed
      - HOLT RICHESON, Admor. of CHARLES SEATON deced., Plt. against MATTHIAS
ABBOTT Deft., On Writ of Scirefacias   The Sheriff having returned that the Defendant is not an Inhabitant of this County, this suit therefore abates by his return

p.   Caroline County Court 11th of March 1773
174   - HOLT RICHESON, Admor. of CHARLES SEATON deced., Plt. against CATHERINE
      FAULKNER Deft. In Case   Came the Plantif by his Attorney and the Defendt.
being arrested failed to appear tho: solemnly called; It is considered by the Court that
unless the said Defendant appear at the next Court and answer this suit, Judgment be
entered against her for what shall appear to be due the Plantif & costs
      - The Same Plt. against BENJAMIN FAULKNER Deft.   In Case
  Came the Plantif by his Attorney and the Defendant being arrested & failing to appear
tho: solemnly called, It is considered by the Court that unless the Defendt. appear at the
next Court and answer this suit, Judgment be entered against him for what shall appear
to be due the Plantif and costs
      - The Same Plt. against JOHN FAULKNER & BENJAMIN FAULKNER Defts. In Case
  Came the Plantif by his Attorney and the Defendant, BENJAMIN, being arrested and
failing to appear tho: solemnly called; It is considered by the Court that unless the
Defendant appear at the next Court and answer this suit, Judgment be entered against
him and CATHERINE FAULKNER, who was security for his appearance, for what shall
appear to be due the Plantif & costs; & the Sherif having returned that the Defendant,
JNO:, is not an Inhabitant of this County, the same is discontinued against him
      - ANDREW COCKRANE & COMPY., Plt. against JOHN LUCAS Deft.   In Case
  Came the Plantif by his Attorney and the former Writ in this suit not being executed,
On motion of the said Plantif by his Attorney, a new Writ is awarded him against the
Defendant returnable to the next Court

- JOHN ALE against HENRY PEMBERTON   On Petition
The Petitioner failing to appear, On motion of the Defendt., Judgment is granted him against the Plt. for his costs in this behalf expended

p.   (This page also is numbered 174)
174   Caroline County Court 11th of March 1773
- ANTHONY McKETTRICK & CO., against ROBERT BILL   On Petition
The Sherif having returned that the Defendant is not an Inhabitant of this County, this suit therefore abates by his return
- RICHARD ROY et Uxor. Plts. against RICHD: WOOLFOLK CHANDLER Deft.
In Case   This suit abates by the Defendants death
- Ordered ROBERT MICKLEBERRY pay JNO: SOUTHWORTH Two hundred & fifty pounds of tobacco for attending this Court ten days as an evidence for him ads: GOODALL
- Ordered ROBERT MICKLEBERRY pay JNO: DUDLEY GEORGE, Two hundred & twenty five pounds of tobacco for attending this Court nine days as an evidence for him ads: GOODALL
- Ordered ROBERT MICKLEBERRY pay BEVERLEY WINSLOW Four hundred & sixty pounds of tobacco for attending this Court four days and three times coming & returning sixty miles as an evidence for him at the suit of GOODALL
- Ordered RICHARD GOODALL pay BENJA: TIMBERLAKE one thousand & sixty pounds of tobacco for attending this Court ten days as an evidence & six times coming & returning Forty five miles as an evidence for him against MICKLEBERRY
- Ordered RICHARD GOODALL pay MICHAEL ANDERSON Four hundred & sixty pounds of tobacco for attending this Court four days and 3 times coming & returning forty miles as an evidence for him against MICKLEBERRY
- WILLIAM JOHN & DAVID CROSSE Plts. against JAMES QUARLES & JOHN QUARLES JUNR., Defts.   Motion on Replevy Bond
The Defendants who had legal notice of this motion being solemnly called failed to appear; On motion of the Plantifs by their Attorney, Judgment is granted them against the said Defendants for One hundred & seventy four poudns three shilings, the Penalty in the said Bond, to be discharged by the payment of Eighty seven pounds one shilling & six pence with legal Interest from the ninth day of September 1772 til paid & costs of this motion
- On the Petition of ROBERT GILCHRIST Gent., ordered that ANTHONY THORNTON, WILLIAM BUCKNER, RICHD. JOHNSON & FRANCIS BUCKNER or any three of them, being first sworn, view the Road petitioned for to be altered by the said ROBERT GILCHRIST and report the conveniences & inconveniences thereof to next Court

p.   Caroline County Court 11th of March 1773
175   - RICHARD GOODALL Plt. against ROBERT MICKLEBURROUGH Deft.   In Case
Came the parties by their Attorneys and a Jury, to wit, RICHARD JOHNSTON foreman &c., being impanneled & sworn well & truly to try the matter on issue joined, do day that the Defendant is Not Guilty of the Breach of Promise in the Declaration mentioned; Therefore it is considered by the Court that the Defendant recover of the Plantif his costs by him about his defence in this suit expended & that the Plantif for his false clamour be in Mercy &c.
- ROBERT GILCHRIST Gent., Plt. against JNO: ALE & JNO: WEBSTER Deffts.
In Case   Pursuant to a Note from under the hands of the Defendants, It is considered by the Court that the Plantif recover against the said Defendants Eight pounds, seven shillings and four pence half penny, with legal Interest from the tenth day of March

1773 till paid, together with his costs in this behalf expended, & the said Defendants in Mercy &c.

    - JOHN BROADDUS Plt. against MARK BOULWARE & ANN BLACKBURN Defts.
  In Case   Came the parties by their Attorneys and the Defendants say they cannot deny the Plantifs action so far as to nine pounds eleven shillings with legal Interest on seven pounds eighteen shillings and eight pence from the eleventh day of March 1773 til paid; Therefore it is considered by the Court that the Plt. recover against the said Defendants the said sum of Nine pounds eleven shillings with legal Interest on the said seven pounds eighteen shillings & eight pence from the eleventh day of March 1773 til paid, by the Defendants in manner & form aforesaid confessed, together with his costs in this behalf expended and the said Defendants in Mercy &c.

    - The Road altered by JAMES TAYLOR Gent., leading through his Plantation is established agreeable thereto

    - HART & MARSHALL Plts. against JAMES HEAD LYNCH Deft. In Case
JNO: THILMAN entered himself Special Bail for the Defendant according to Law

p.   <u>Caroline County Court 11th of March 1773</u>
176   - Messrs. GLASFORD & HENDERSON Plts. against JOHN THILMAN Deft. In Debt
    - Came as well the Plantifs by their Attorney as the Defendant in his proper person, and the said Defendant saith he cannot deny the Plts. action; Therefore it is considered by the Court that the Plantifs recover against the said Defendant Three hundred & fourteen pounds ten shillings and one penny, the Debt in the Declaration specified, together with their costs by them in this behalf expended; and the said Defendant in Mercy &c., But this Judgment except the costs is to be discharged by the payment of One hundred & fifty seven pounds five shillings & half penny with legal Interest on One hundred and fifty pounds part thereof from the first day of October 1770 til paid and the remainder with legal Interest from the first of June 1771 til paid, deducting seventeen pounds ten shillings & four pence half penny paid fifteenth day of September 1772

    - ANN WALLER against WILLIAM SMITHER   On Petition
The Defendant being duly summoned and failing to appear; On motion of the Petitioner by her Attorney, Judgment is granted her against the said Defendant for two pounds, the Debt in the Petition specified, also her costs in this behalf expended

    - HOLT RICHESON, Admor: of CHARLES SEATON deced., Plt. against JOSEPH PRICE
  Deft. On Writ of Scirefacias   Came the Plantif by his Attorney and the former Writ in this suit not being executed; On motion of the said Plantif a new Writ is awarded him against the Defendant returnable to the next Court

    - DUNCAN GRAHAM against LAZARUS YARBROUGH   On Petition
Came the Plantif by his Attorney and the Defendant being duly summoned and failing to appear tho: solemnly called; Therefore it is considered by the Court that the Petitioner recover against the said Defendant one pound fourteen shillings, Eighty pounds of nett tobacco & seven shillings & six pence, the Debt in the Petition specified; also his costs in this behalf expended

p.   <u>Caroline County Court 11th of March 1773</u>
177   - JAMES FLETCHER against WILLIAM REYNOLDS   On Petition
Came the Petitioner by his Attorney and the Defendant being duly summoned failed to appear tho: solemnly called; Therefore it is considered by the Court that the Petitioner recover against the said Defendant two pounds six shilllings, the Debt in the Petition specified; also his costs in this behalf expended

- THOMAS BROWN against WILLIAM BROWN JR.   On Petition
The Defendant being duly summoned failed to appear tho: solemnly called; On motion
of the Petitioner by his Attorney, Judgment is granted him against the said Defendt. for
one pound ten shillings with legal Inteest from the tenth day of July 1772 till paid; also
his costs in this behalf expended
     - YOUNGER PITTS Plt. against HENRY MARTIN & JAS: LOVERN Defts. In Debt
Came the Plantif by his Attorney and the Defendants being arrested failed to appear
tho: solemnly called. It is considered by the Court that unless the Defendants appear at
the next Court and answer this suit, Judgment be entered against them & ISRAEL SNEED
who was security for their appearance, for what shall appear to be due the Plantif &
costs
     - JOSEPH BOHANNON, Admor. of MAJOR LEFON deced., against JOSEPH McGHEE &
JOHN TURNER   On Petition   Came the Petitioner by his Attorney and the former
Process not being executed, On motion of the said Petitioner a new summons is awarded
him against the said Defendt: returnable to the next Court
     - JOHN MOUNTAGUE Plt. against FREDERICK FORTSON, Deft.   In Case
On motion of the Plantif by his Attorney, Judgment is granted him against the said
Defendant for his costs in this behalf expended

p   Caroline County Court 11th of March 1773
178   - WILLIAM BOWLER Plt. against THOMAS HACKETT Deft.   Trespass Assault &
     Battery   On motion of lthe Plantif by his Attorney, Judgment is granted
him against the said Defendant for his costs in this behalf expended.
     - Ordered JOHN WATTS with his gang assist ROBERT WOOLFOLK & his gang in
repairing the Road from the DOUGE TOWN BRIDGE to HOOMES's PLANTATION
     - Ordered the Court be adjourn'd till the Court in Course
     - The Minutes of the preceeding Orders were signed by
                    ANTHONY THORNTON Gent.

(The remainder of this page is blank.)

(Caroline County Order Book 1772-1776, will be continued in a subsequent publication beginning
on page 179 with the Court held on Friday, March the Twelfth 1773)

ABBOTT. James 39; Jatthias 87
 William 32, 39.
ACREY. John 6.
ALCOCK. Fanney 39; Thomas 39, 40, 42,
 53, 60.
ALE. John 8; William Junr. 4.
ALEXANDER. John 1; John Junr. 1.
ALLEN. Thomas 34.
ALSOP. Benjamin 29, 40, 47, 84; George 9, 85.
ANDERSON. Batlett (Exr. of Harry Bobinson) 29;
 Garland 51; Michael 88; Thomas 87;
 Walter 58.
ANOMY. Henry (deced.-72).
ARMISTEAD. Henry 74; John (Gent. Justice -2),
 5, 6, 12, 24, 37, 47, 56, (Presented -80).
ARNOLD. Anthony 15; William 40, 54.
ASHBURN. John (deced. -40); Mary (Exrx. of
 John, deced.) 40; Molly 6, 23, 40.
ATKINS. Elizabeth 84.
ATKISON. George 77, 79.
AYLETT. William 12.
AYRES. William 53.

BABER. Francis 43, 73; James 31.
BAINE. Alexander 5, 62.
BAKER. Benjamin 6.
BALL. Ben: 59.
BARBY. John 25, 68.
BARKSDALE. DAniel 11, 16, 40, 45, 49, 67,
 76, 77.
BARLOW. William 69.
BATTAILE. Lawrence 15, 69.
BAUGHAN/BOUGHAN. Benjamin 3, 83;
 Dorothy 83; Hundley 58.
BAYLOR. John 37, 38; John (Esqr., 3),
 (deced.-12), 86; John (Admr. of John Baylor
 Esqr. deced.) 86.
BAYNHAM. John 42, 61, 76, 85, 86.
BEADLES. James 78.
BEAZLEY. Charles (deced., Inventory returned
 -76).
BELL. James 50; John 59; Thomas 30.
BENSON. John 59.
BERRY. Thomas 32.
BEVERIDGE. John 18.
BEVERLEY. Harry 26, 33, 47, 49, 77, 79.
BIGG. Robert Fleming 27.
BILL. Robert 88.
BILLUPS/BILLOPS. John 30, 56.

BLACKBURN. Ambrose 11; Ann 50, 89;
 Elias (deced.-11), (See Mary Fletcher); 77.
BLADES. William 74.
BLANTON. Richard 51.
BOGLE, SCOTT & CO. -18, 53, 65.
BOHANNON. Joseph (Admr. of Major Lefon,
 deced) 90.
BOULWARE. Mark 89.
BOURNE. John 17.
BOUTWELL,. John 39, 42; John Junr. 41.
BOWCOCK. Anthony & Betty (Exr. & Exrx. of
 James Bowcock, deced.) 10, 63, 64;
 Edward 29; John 13.
BOWIE. James 38; James Junr. 3, 30, 54, 57, 58,
 (Gent.-76), 78.
BOWLER. William 25, 26, 40, 44, 45, 82, 90.
BOYD. David 27; Spencer 53, 55.
BRAIME/BRAME. Melchisedeck 31, 38, 61, 70,
 73, 74.
BRAND. John 16, 83, 84.
BRANSOME. John 25.
BRASFIELD. Edward 71; Elizabeth 71.
BRIDGES: Burks 80; Douge Town 90;
 Guineas 38, 39; Marrococick 76; Pamunkey
 River 69, 83; Pewmansend 83.
BROADDUS. John 17, 52, 74, 89.
BROUGHILL. John 8, 10; William 8, 56.
BROWN. Daniel 58; John 9, 54, 84;
 Mary & William (Exrs. of John Brown, deced.) 5,
 8, 29; Mrs. 84; Thomas 30, 90; William 31;
 William Junr. 43, 55, 56, 74, 77, 79, 90;
 William Senr. 30, 47, 49, 53.
BRUMSKILL. John (deced.-61); William (deced.
 -61), (See William Harris).
BUCKNER. Elizabeth 77; Francis 39, 88;
 George 77; Jane 48; John (Gent.-3), 21, (Gent.
 Justice -37), 38, 75, 77; Mordecai (Gent.-17),
 25, 38; Richard (Militia Capt. -86); Thomas 20,
 21, 51; Thomas (Gent., deced. -77);
 William (Gent. Justice -2), 39, 77, (Ordinary
 -81), 88; William Junr. (Gent.-13), 40, 57, 65.
BULLARD. George 26; John 15, 20.
BURETT. Humphrey 75.
BURK. Henry 33, 51, 65, 70; Thomas 7, 10, 15,
 20, 23, 31, 33, 39, 51, 58, 65-67, 70, 71, 73.
BURNLEY. Zachariah 40.
BURNLEY & BRACKENRIDGE. -5, 41.
BURRUS -71; Jacob 31, (Presnted -79), 81;
 Samuel 70, 76, 83.

DIXON (contd.) Edward & John Skinker, (Exrs.
   of Thomas Turner, deced.-36; Richard 77;
   William 71.
DONOHOE. Michael 37.
DOODY. Joseph 12.
DOWNER. John 6, 23, 40.
DUDLEY. Ambrose 21; William 7, 25, 61, 67,
   74, 78, 85.
DULING. Larkin 82.
DUNLOP. James 17, 26, (Gent.-69), 70, 76, 81,
   85; & Co. 23; & Crosse 46, 49, 55, 56, 74, 87.
DURRETT. Francis 18; Henry 32; John 32, 77;
   Richard 21.
DUVAL. James 39.

EDMONDSON. Humphrey 55.
ELLIOTT. Benjamin 30.
ELLISS. Augustin (deced.-70), 71; John 38.
EMMERSON. Elizabeth 68; Elliot 15, 31, 65;
   James 6; Patty 31.
ESTIS. John 71, 75; Philip 80.
EUBANK. George 80; William 71.
EVANS. John 14, 71.

FARISH. Fanny 76; James 66, 76;
   Robert 27, 71; Sarah (deced., Inventory
   returned -38).
FAULKNER. Benjamin 38, 87; Catherine 87;
   John 87; Johnson 86.
FENINGHOLTZ. Jacob 52, 53.
FERGUSON/FARGUSON. John 8, 15, 30, 62;
   Robert 7, 26, 49.
FIELDS. John 55.
FITZHUGH -77; William (Esqr.-42) 71.
FLEET. William 4, 20-22, 29, 32, 33, 66.
FLEMING. Francis 15, 25, 50, 57, 67.
FLETCHER. James 11, 31; Mary 11;
   Mary (Exrx. of Elias Blackburn, deced.) 19, 69.
FLIPPO. William 1, 40.
FORTSON. Frederick 5-7, 9, 12, 20, 27, 33,
   37, 38, 51, 58, 66, 67, 70, 76, 90;
   Stephen 5, 7, 33, 37, 55, 70, 76.
FORTUNE. Elizabeth (Presented -80);
   Richard 48.
FOX. Ann (Admrx. of William Fox, deced.) 76;
   William (deced-76); William 32, (Mariner -58)
FULCHER. William 41.
FURLONG -62.

GAINES. Daniel (Gent.-81); George 23, 38;
   John 33; Thomas 17.
GALE. Mathew (Presented -79); Matthew Junr. 19.
GARNETT. Delphia 83; Delphia (Widow of
   Larkin -43); James 72; Larkin (deced. -43),
   (Inventory returned -83); Muscoe & Co. 10, 63;
   Muscoe (Exr. of James Garnett, deced.) 36;
   Thomas (Admr. of Larkin Garnett, deced.) 43.
GARROTT. John 21; Mary 43;
   Robert 19, 20, 32, 40, 43, 65.
GATEWOOD. James Junr. 22; John 20, 66, 71;
   Joseph 17, 18, 39, 51; Reubin 39, 51.
GAUNT. James 20, 22, 64, 65; Joseph (deced.-53)
   (Inventory returned -76); Sarah (Admrx. of
   Joseph Gaunt, deced.) 53; William 68, 71.
GEORGE. Frances 69; John 4, 15, 16, 20, 29, 31,
   33-35, 42, 52, 63, 66, 69, 84; John Junr. 42;
   John Dudley 88; Lodowich 35, 61;
   Reuben 76, 84; Richard 33, 35.
GIBSON. George 14, 55.
GILCHRIST. Robert (Gent. Justice -3), 5, 19, 20,
   23, 24, 30, 31, 37-39, 41, 43, 45-47, 67, 70, 71,
   76, 77, 81, 83, 85, 88; Robert Exr. of John
   Miller, deced.) 48.
GIMBOW. James 26, 68.
GLANTON. Benjamin 1, 40; Jonathan 51.
GLASSELL. John 39, 54.
GLASSFORD & HENDERSON. Messrs. 89.
GOALDER. Elizabeth 60.
GOBURN. George 75.
GODBEY. George 43; Russell 43.
GOODALL. Charles (deced.-1), 26, 40, 50;
   James (deced.-86), 87; Park 31; Richard 30,
   35, 50, 53, 57, 61, 82, 84, 88; William 26, 43,
   55, (Presented -79); William (of Province of
   Georgia -86).
GOODLOE. Henry 52.
GOODRICH. John 12, 19, 26, 50, 74.
GORDON. Charles 33; Samuel 51.
GOULDMAN. Richard 19.
GOVAN. Archibald 54, 62; James 68, 82.
GRADY. John 57; Joshua 77.
GRAHAM. Duncan 89; John & Co. -1.
GRAVATT. Elliss 56.
GRAVES. Benjamin 34; William 15.
GRAY. John & Co. 12, 23, 38, 47, 55, 65, 69,
   72, 73.
GREGORY. James 9, 38.
GRIFFIN. John 14, 20, 23, 27, 54, 57, 62-64, 83;
   Roy 32, 71.

GRIFFIS. John 79.
GRUMBLEY. John 31.
GRYMES. Philip (Gent.-32); William 63.
GUTHRIE. William 13.
GUY. George 12, (Gent.-24), (Gent. Justice -37),
41, 42, 49, 51, 61, 62, 67, 70, 74, 85, 86;
George (Admr. of Farrell & Ann Hughes, deced.)
20, 33, 66, 67.

HACKETT -77; Garrett 14, 25, 31, 32, 57, 60, 79;
John (deced.-39), 49; Susanna (Widow of John
Hackett, deced.-39); Thomas 52, 90.
HACKNEY. William 32.
HADEN. Anthony 8, 62.
HALBERT. Francis 70; Martha 70.
HALEY. Humphrey 33, 83; John (deced., Will
further proved -40), (Inventory returned -42);
Thomas 20, 66; William 75.
HALL. Ro: (deced.-46).
HAMPTON. John 41, 80.
HARGRAVE/HARGROVE. Samuel 2, 41, 69, 83.
HARRIS. John 44, 56, 74; William & Robert
Scott (Exrs. of Wm. Brumskill, deced.) 61.
HARRISON. Andrew 1, 2, 16, 25; Leonard 24,
67; William 2, 8, 16, 54, 67, 79.
HART. Ann 19, 42; & Marshall 82, 89;
Robert 61, 78, 85.
HARVEY. John 23, 34, 67, 85.
HAWES. Isaac 27, 84; Samuel (Gent. Justice -4),
6, 42, 71, 77; Samuel Junr. (Gent.-17).
HAYNES. Ann 50.
HAYES/HAYS. Daniel 37, 79.
HERNDON. David 8; Edward 85; Hannah 3, 4;
Hannah (Exr. of James Herndon, deced.) 23, 68;
John 87; Reuben 18, 34.
HEWITT. John 32, 71, 74-77, 81; William 80, 87.
HIGGIN. William 5; William Junr. 62.
HILL. John (Gent. -12).
HILTON. William 37.
HIPKINS. 1John (Militia Ensign -86); LeeRoy 2,
5, 7, 11, 16, 53; LeeRoy & Samuel (Exrs. of
Samuel Hipkins, deced.) 9, 15, 63;
Richard 1, 17, 54; Samuel (deced. -9).
HOBBS. Benjamin 22.
HOE. Seymour 86.
HOLLAWAY. Betty 39; Charles 39;
George (deced., Will proved -39); Nathan 17.
HOLLIDAY. John 13, 16.
HOOMES. Joseph (an Infant) 57.
HORD. Thomas 25; William 19, 25, 51.

HOUSTON. Hugh (Exr. of William Houston, deced.)
15; Robert 43; William (deced. -15).
HUBBARD. Benjamin 2, 13, (Gent.-21), 26, 45,
46, 48, 68, 73, 78, (Presented -80), 86.
HUBBARD & BAKER. -6.
HUDDLESTON. Cornelius 7; John 62.
HUGHES (deced.-20); (See George Guy), 20;
Farrell (deced. -20), (See George Guy) 20.
HUNDEN. Reuben 62.
HUNDLEY. Jacob 58.
HUNT. Edward 29.
HUNTER. William (deced. -69).
HURT. Agnis 82; Benjamin 83; Elizabeth 82;
James 10; James (deced. -4), 82;
Titus (deced. -83).

INNIS. Robert (deced. -69.
ISBELL. Ann (Exrs. of Daniel Isbell, deced.) 44;
Benjamin 10; Daniel (deced. -44); George 77;
James 31.

JAMESON. James (deced.-52); Mary (Admrx. of
James Jameson, deced.) 52.
JERDINE. Robert 54.
JERVICE. Aaron 18, 22, 65; Richard 13, 20, 26,
58, 66, 68; Thomas 34.
JESSE. John 27.
JETER. Ambrose 32; John 1, 21, 71.
JETT. Thomas (Gent.-5), 6.
JOHN. William 88.
JOHNSTON/JOHNSON. Aquila 60, 71, 75;
Benjamin 8, 31, 33, 43, 53; Caty 83; Clara 76;
Daniel 76; Elizabeth 76; James 10-12, 23, 56,
63, 64, 67, 81; Jeddiah 80; John 2, 12, 27, 40,
42, 44, 55, 76; Margaret 2. Philip 23, (Gent.
-74); Philip (Admr. of Thomas Johnston, deced)
8, 23, 67; Richard 11, 22, 40, 50, 54, 55, 66, 74,
76, 88; Richard (Exr. of Francis Coleman, deced)
10, 13-15, 18, 23, 36, 62, 64, 65, 70, 85;
Robert 59; Robert & Benjamin (Exrs. of William
Johnston, deced.) 12, 39, 58, 67; Thomas (deced.
-35); William 12, 16, 17 19, 46, 47, 69, 74;
William (Doctor) 10, 14, 16, 24, 48, 58, 70;
William (deced. -1), 43.
JONES. Edmund 9, 74; John 12, 29, 73, 79;
Joseph 25, (Gent.-68); Lewis 83; Micajah 9,
38; Philip 1; Thomas 2; William 9.
JOUITT. John 72.
JUSTICES (and first appearance as Justice) John
Armistead -2; John Buckner -37; (contd.)

WOODFORD. William 3, 37, (Gent. Justice -45), 69, 70, 75.
WOOLFOLK. John 84; John (deced. -53); Joseph (deced.-77); Richard 4, 38, 71; Robert 12, 30, 31, 37, 38, 58, 73, 84, 90; Robert Junr. 29, 36.
WORTHAM. Samuel (Gent. -69), 76.
WREN. Mary 17.
WRIGHT. James 12, 17; John 2, 75; Robert 48.
WYAT(T). Richard 31, 73, 74.

YARBROUGH -86; James 35, 42; Lazarous 17, 89.
YATES. George 38, 40, 71, 75, 77 Michael 40.
YOUNG. -71; Catesby 77; John 51, (Presented -79), 83; Margaret 77, 82; Nathaniel 76; Richard 46; William 70, 83.

ZACHARY. Peter 59.

Heritage Books by Ruth and Sam Sparacio:

Lancaster County, Virginia Order Book, 1695–1699

Lancaster County, Virginia Order Book, 1699–1701

Lancaster County, Virginia Order Book, 1701–1703

Lancaster County, Virginia Order Book, 1703–1706

Lancaster County, Virginia Order Book, 1732–1736

Lancaster County, Virginia Will Book, 1675–1689

Loudoun County, Virginia Order Book, 1763–1764

Loudoun County, Virginia Order Book, 1764

Louisa County, Virginia Deed Book, 1744–1746

Louisa County, Virginia Order Book, 1742–1744

Madison County, Virginia Deed Book Abstracts, 1793–1804

Madison County, Virginia Deed Book, 1793–1813, and Marriage Bonds, 1793–1800

Middlesex County, Virginia Deed Book, 1679–1688

Middlesex County, Virginia Deed Book, 1688–1694

Middlesex County, Virginia Deed Book, 1694–1703

Middlesex County, Virginia Deed Book, 1703–1709

Middlesex County, Virginia Deed Book, 1709–1720

Middlesex County, Virginia Order Book, 1686–1690

Middlesex County, Virginia Record Book, 1721–1813

Northumberland County, Virginia Deed and Will Book, 1650–1655

Northumberland County, Virginia Deed and Will Book, 1655–1658

Northumberland County, Virginia Deed and Will Book, 1662–1666

Northumberland County, Virginia Deed and Will Book, 1666–1670

Northumberland County, Virginia Deed and Will Book, 1670–1672 and 1706–1711

Northumberland County, Virginia Deed and Will Book, 1711–1712

Northumberland County, Virginia Order Book, 1652–1657

Northumberland County, Virginia Order Book, 1657–1661

Northumberland County, Virginia Order Book, 1665–1669

Northumberland County, Virginia Order Book, 1669–1673

Northumberland County, Virginia Order Book, 1680–1683

Northumberland County, Virginia Order Book, 1683–1686

Northumberland County, Virginia Order Book, 1699–1700

Northumberland County, Virginia Order Book, 1700–1702

Northumberland County, Virginia Order Book, 1702–1704

Orange County, Virginia Deeds, 1743–1759

Orange County, Virginia Order Book Abstracts 1747–1748

Orange County, Virginia Order Book Abstracts 1752–1753

Prince William County, Virginia Deed Book, 1749–1752

Prince William County, Virginia Order Book Abstracts, 1752–1753

Prince William County, Virginia Order Book Abstracts, 1753–1757

(Old) Rappahannock County, Virginia Deed and Will Book Abstracts, 1656–1662

(Old) Rappahannock County, Virginia Deed and Will Book Abstracts, 1662–1665

(Old) Rappahannock County, Virginia Deed and Will Book Abstracts, 1663–1668

(Old) Rappahannock County, Virginia Deed and Will Book Abstracts, 1665–1677

(Old) Rappahannock County, Virginia Deed and Will Book Abstracts, 1668–1670

(Old) Rappahannock County, Virginia Deed and Will Book Abstracts, 1670–1672

(Old) Rappahannock County, Virginia Deed and Will Book Abstracts, 1672–1673/4

(Old) Rappahannock County, Virginia Deed and Will Book Abstracts, 1673/4–1676

(Old) Rappahannock County, Virginia Deed and Will Book Abstracts, 1677–1678/9

(Old) Rappahannock County, Virginia Deed and Will Book Abstracts, 1678/9–1682

(Old) Rappahannock County, Virginia Deed and Will Book Abstracts, 1682–1686

(Old) Rappahannock County, Virginia Deed and Will Book Abstracts, 1686–1688

(Old) Rappahannock County, Virginia Deed and Will Book Abstracts, 1688–1692

(Old) Rappahannock County, Virginia Order Book Abstracts, 1683–1685

(Old) Rappahannock County, Virginia Order Book, 1689–1692

(Old) Rappahannock County, Virginia Will Book, 1682–1687

Richmond County, Virginia Deed Book Abstracts, 1692–1695

Richmond County, Virginia Deed Book Abstracts, 1695–1701

Richmond County, Virginia Deed Book Abstracts, 1701–1704

Richmond County, Virginia Deed Book Abstracts, 1705–1708

Richmond County, Virginia Deed Book Abstracts, 1708–1711

Richmond County, Virginia Deed Book Abstracts, 1711–1714

Richmond County, Virginia Deed Book Abstracts, 1715–1718

Richmond County, Virginia Deed Book Abstracts, 1718–1719

Richmond County, Virginia Deed Book Abstracts, 1719–1721

Richmond County, Virginia Deed Book Abstracts, 1721–1725

Richmond County, Virginia Order Book Abstracts, 1694–1697

Richmond County, Virginia Order Book Abstracts, 1697–1699

Richmond County, Virginia Order Book abstracts, 1699–1701

Richmond County, Virginia Order Book Abstracts, 1714–1715

Richmond County, Virginia Order Book Abstracts, 1719–1721

Richmond County, Virginia Order Book, 1692–1694

Richmond County, Virginia Order Book, 1702–1704

Richmond County, Virginia Order Book, 1717–1718

Richmond County, Virginia Order Book, 1718–1719

Spotsylvania County, Virginia Deed Book, 1722–1725

Spotsylvania County, Virginia Deed Book, 1725–1728

Spotsylvania County, Virginia Deed Book: 1730–1731

Spotsylvania County, Virginia Order Book Abstracts, 1742–1744

Spotsylvania County, Virginia Order Book Abstracts, 1744–1746

Stafford County, Virginia Deed and Will Book, 1686–1689

Stafford County, Virginia Deed and Will Book, 1689–1693

Stafford County, Virginia Deed and Will Book, 1699–1709

Stafford County, Virginia Deed and Will Book, 1780–1786, and Scheme Book Orders, 1790–1793

Stafford County, Virginia Deed Book, 1722–1728 and 1755–1765

Stafford County, Virginia Order Book, 1664–1668 and 1689–1690

Stafford County, Virginia Order Book, 1691–1692

Stafford County, Virginia Order Book, 1692–1693

Stafford County, Virginia Will Book, 1729–1748

Stafford County, Virginia Will Book, 1748–1767

Westmoreland County, Virginia Deed and Will Abstracts, 1723–1726

Westmoreland County, Virginia Deed and Will Abstracts, 1726–1729

Westmoreland County, Virginia Deed and Will Abstracts, 1729–1732

Westmoreland County, Virginia Deed and Will Abstracts, 1732–1734

Westmoreland County, Virginia Deed and Will Abstracts, 1734–1736

Westmoreland County, Virginia Deed and Will Abstracts, 1736–1740

Westmoreland County, Virginia Deed and Will Abstracts, 1740–1742

Westmoreland County, Virginia Deed and Will Abstracts, 1742–1745

Westmoreland County, Virginia Deed and Will Abstracts, 1745–1747

Westmoreland County, Virginia Deed and Will Abstracts, 1747–1748

Westmoreland County, Virginia Deed and Will Abstracts, 1749–1751

Westmoreland County, Virginia Deed and Will Abstracts, 1751–1754

Westmoreland County, Virginia Deed and Will Abstracts, 1754–1756

Westmoreland County, Virginia Order Book, 1705–1707

Westmoreland County, Virginia Order Book, 1707–1709

Westmoreland County, Virginia Order Book, 1709–1712

www.ingramcontent.com/pod-product-compliance
Lightning Source LLC
Chambersburg PA
CBHW080001280326
41935CB00013B/1709